THERE'S TROUBLE IN THE TEA-LEAVES

There's Trouble in the Tea-Leaves

A light-hearted account of Blackouts, Bombs and Barrage Balloons in a Cornish Village

Betty Kellar

ISIS
LARGE PRINT
Oxford

First published in Great Britain 1998
by United Writers Publications Ltd

Published in Large Print 2002 by ISIS Publishing Ltd,
7 Centremead, Osney Mead, Oxford OX2 0ES
by arrangement with United Writers Publications Ltd

British Library Cataloguing in Publication Data
Kellar, Betty
    There's Trouble in the Tea-Leaves. – Large print ed. –
(ISIS reminiscence series)
    1. World War, 1939–1945 – Personal narratives, British
    2. World War, 1939–1945 – Social aspects – England
    – Cornwall
    3. Large type books
    4. Cornwall (England) – History
    I. Title
    940.5'3161'092

ISBN 0–7531–9802–9 (hb)
ISBN 0–7531–9803–7 (pb)

Printed and bound by Antony Rowe, Chippenham

To Alan, my husband, for all his help and encouragement, and in particular, for taking over on the word-processor.

Preface

All the events in this book are true, as far as my memory serves me — even if it has not, the odds are favourable because wherever possible I checked contemporary newspapers, now stored on micro-film in Plymouth Reference Library. I am very grateful to the helpful staff who work there. Also to those wartime reporters of the *Western Morning News* and *Evening Herald* whose work is preserved for future generations to study.

The characters in the book all existed, though I have changed their names and jumbled them up. So no one will be able to say, "That's my Grandma she's talking about," though they might be able to say, "Mrs. P. sounds like a bit of my Gran, a bit more of her next-door neighbour and a lot of old Miss—? up the hill."

I have not altered anything about my own family. My sisters are quite happy at my tales of them, and I know my Mum would have been. I only hope Gan is! and that she is not glaring at me from the Other Side.

The Cornish Periphery of Plymouth

CHAPTER
ONE

'When constabulary duty's to be done
A policeman's lot is not a happy one.'
(*Gilbert and Sullivan*)

The day we moved from Millpool Head to West Street, our furniture piled high on Mr Dobson's rag-and-bone handcart, was a highlight in my life. It was the first time I remember feeling important.

My Mother and Grandmother (Gan) followed directly behind the cart. Gan marched straight-backed, her nose in the air, firmly gripping an old leather suitcase in one hand and a bag of crockery in the other, while Mum leaned the push-chair up the hill, two-year-old Jill inside it and Diane, at seven, a year younger than me, hanging onto the handle. Feeling like Anna, who carried the banner, I walked at the back, carrying the cat.

Gan had had a furious row with Mr Dobson when he arrived to collect our belongings at eight o'clock that morning. He wanted to take the shorter and flatter route to our new home, along the village's main street.

Her temper always on a short fuse, Gan had expostulated, "It should be what your customers want, not you!"

1

"Not if it's up that hill and twice the distance," the rag-and-bone man had retorted. "Not likely, Missus."

If it hadn't been for Mum's placatory words and an extra one-and-sixpence, I think he would have dumped our furniture off his cart and left us to it.

So he took us, in a dignified silence which matched Gan's, up the longer and hillier road skirting the village, to arrive at our new abode with no more than three or four interested pairs of eyes watching our progress from behind curtained cottage windows, when it could have been the whole of West Street.

Gan might have been simmering beneath her air of hauteur, with my gentle mother slightly apologetic for having saved the situation, but I was conscious of nothing but excitement. I waved proudly to Mrs Finchcombe, out on her doorstep to collect her milk, and nearly lost the cat. But not even Gan's familiar admonition, rapped sharply over her shoulder to "Stop showing off, Betty!" flattened me as it usually did. Pushing Winkle firmly back into the peg-bag from which he was struggling to escape, I trotted behind the little cavalcade, revelling in the undoubted interest of curtain-twitching neighbours as we passed by.

Though the terraced house in West Street was much better than the tiny old cottage in Millpool Head, we hadn't moved simply to better our living conditions. We couldn't afford to, and only sheer desperation had made Mum and Gan eventually decide to abandon a rent of three-and-sixpence a week, and take on a seemingly astronomical one of six shillings.

We had left Plymouth in 1937, after my father died when he was only thirty-two, to live in this remote Cornish village. Mum had been left with two children, another on the way, and no more than the statutory ten shillings a week widow's pension, with a six shillings child allowance. It was then that my Grandmother came to live with us, bringing with her a widow's pension from the First World War, which undoubtedly saved us from being split up.

The cottage was very dilapidated, with neither water nor electricity. We used an oil lamp and cooked on an ancient stove, and had to get water from a communal tap at the end of a long yard in front of the cottages. The single lavatory, which served the row of four cottages, was at the same end as the tap.

Despite all this, Mum and Gan had at first thought themselves fortunate to find this cottage. That was before they became familiar with Mrs Murdoch.

Mrs Murdoch, who was our next door neighbour, was mentally retarded, but the knowledge that she couldn't help her behaviour did not make our position any easier to bear. She spat on our windows, threw rotten apples at us from her bedroom window, and loudly abused us whenever we chanced to meet.

It was not to be expected that Gan would be able to take this, and she firmly told Mrs Murdoch a few home truths which that lady was quite unable to accept. The result was a dreadful slanging match between the two women, during which Diane and I were only too thankful to obey Gan's sharp order to 'get back into the house'. Mum bravely stayed out in the yard, trying to defuse the indefusible, for she could not make her voice heard above the furiously traded insults of the two protagonists.

It ended when Gan was worn out and came in, slamming the door behind her.

"That's it," she announced, breathing heavily. "We're getting out of this house and away from that infernal woman."

But Mrs Murdoch got in the last blow. The following morning PC Polworthy called to see us. Beneath his calm and authoritative air, he was at first slightly apologetic.

"I've had a complaint concerning you, Mrs Cooper, which I am bound to investigate," he began.

Gan allowed him to get no further. "Yes, and I've got a complaint too," she snapped. "I suppose it's that cockeyed woman next door. She's made our lives a misery since we came to live here. She ought to be locked away."

Ignoring her interruption, PC Polworthy said, "Mrs Murdoch has made a serious allegation regarding your upstairs window. I wonder if you would mind . . ."

"Upstairs? It was the downstairs window. And if she expected me to believe her cock and bull tale that a bird did it, she must think I'm as potty as she is."

A startled expression had begun to widen the policeman's prominent blue eyes. "A bird," he slowly repeated. "A pigeon, do you mean?"

A disbelieving snort clearly expressed Gan's feelings. "A pigeon? If I'd seen a flock of them flying over the roof I wouldn't have believed her. I know spittle when I see it."

Understanding dawned on the policeman's face. "Are you accusing Mrs Murdoch of spitting on your window, Mrs Cooper?"

"I jolly well am. We've all seen it," and Gan's hot gaze swept to Mum, still standing open-mouthed at the table, a bread-knife in her hand. Diane and I just sat and ate our smoky pieces of toast, rescued by Gan, with a 'damn and blast', after it had fallen off her toasting fork into the fire. It had received its usual perfunctory scrape just before PC Polworthy's knock on the door. We all hastily supported her. Her eyes shot back to the policeman. "So what's the old biddy accusing us of then?" she demanded.

There was an unmistakable gleam of amusement in the man's face. "Something a little more serious than spitting, Mrs Cooper. Mrs Murdoch says you were shining a light through your upstairs blackout, signalling to enemy aircraft."

It took a while before Gan's indignation found its relief in a resigned guffaw. The village policeman was well aware of our neighbour's mental state, accepting it without interference as long as she did no real harm. This was in the days before social workers.

Mr Dobson was sweating by the time he had pushed his cart over the brow of the hill and trundled it round the sharply narrow bend of Dodbrook, into the top end of West Street. He was a big, burly man, dark like a gypsy, his shirt sleeves rolled up to reveal bulging muscles covered in black hair up to his elbows. He unloaded our iron bedsteads, two rolled flock mattresses, a folding table with four kitchen chairs, bits of old carpet and a bag of miscellany, and held out a grimy hand for his money.

Though Gan and he parted on less than friendly terms, it did not stop her from employing him again later, when we acquired a second-hand bed-chair and some more old carpet from a selling-up in the village.

My elation was quashed as soon as Gan had seen off the rag-and-bone man and caught sight of me with the cat, now in my arms.

"Trust you to walk through the streets like Lady Muck," she hissed at me. "Put that plaguey cat out in the garden and do something useful."

Like the rabbit I normally was, I scurried to obey her.

CHAPTER
TWO

'If you don't have a shelter, sit under the stairs.'
(*Government Advice*)

I was as excited as everybody else as we went from
room to room, inspecting our new home. It was the
first time Diane and I had seen it and even to our
childish eyes, it all looked better than No. 3, Millpool
Head.

The wallpaper in the one living-room, a mauve
and white flowered stripe, was well stuck on,
with none of the peeling strips or darkened
shades of rising damp to which we had been
accustomed.

Winding stairs led to a small, dark bedroom at the
front of the house, an even smaller and darker room at
the back.

But they were visions of airiness after the mustard-
painted murkiness of the room we had slept in
the previous night. And looking out of the window, we
discovered the joy of our own lavatory in the little
backyard at the foot of steep, stone steps leading to
the long back garden.

Cooking was done in the living-room, on a kitchen
range which filled one wall. There was no electricity but
we had never had it since leaving Plymouth. Every

night at dusk, Gan lit our tall, brass oil-lamp and to us, the familiar smell of its fumes was part of the deep satisfaction of at last being able to see what we were doing, after an hour spent in the half-light, saving paraffin.

Behind the living-room was what Gan called the wash-house. It contained a copper boiler in which to do the washing, with a deep stone sink beside the back door.

To Mum and Gan, the deepest bliss was having a supply of water in the house, but to us children, it was the change itself.

We had a number of visitors in that first week in our new home, much to Gan's disgust. She had a strong aversion to anyone 'getting in' and invariably when there was a knock on the door, she would peer from behind the curtains before deciding whether to answer it. Mr Brown, the ARP warden, who lived in the house opposite, came the day we moved in. She let him in after the usual vetting. He had come to inspect our blackout.

We had already had a visit from Mr Brown at Millpool Head when he had come to fit our gas masks, an occasion which was highlighted by Mrs Murdoch going slightly berserk and locking herself in her bedroom, to shout abuse down at the unfortunate man.

He never did get into her house, so perhaps she would have done the same as Mrs Pendennis, her other-side neighbour, had threatened to do.

"If we gets gas dropped on us, I'm not putting on these new-fangled things," Mrs Pendennis had declared, her three chins shaking as she laughed at her own facetiousness. "I'll get me head down into the lavvy, and nothing old Hitler can send will get past that." Though I don't know what she thought everyone else would do, with only one lavvy between us.

Mr Brown was deaf, which must have caused him problems when the raids started. He could lip-read though, so it was essential that people caught his eye before speaking to him.

After approving our blackout curtains, which were the same ones we had used at Millpool Head, he looked round the room and asked, "Have you given any thought to where you could shelter in an air-raid?"

Gan said, "Well, I know we're advised to get into the cupboard under the stairs, but ours is too small."

Mr Brown's searching eyes had found the cupboard. "The Government suggest under the stairs, but some of the village cupboards are very small. Mind if I have a look, Mrs Cooper?"

Down on his hands and knees, and missing the eloquent look Gan directed at Mum, Mr Brown got inside the cupboard as far as his head and shoulders. He emerged faster than he went in.

"There's a funny smell in there, Mrs Cooper," he remarked.

Always quick to take offence, Gan retorted, "Well, it was here when we came."

The warden struggled to his feet. "I don't reckon it would do your family's health any good in there."

Gan was beginning to stiffen, the outraged expression on her face one everybody recognised except Mr Brown, who must have been short-sighted as well as deaf. He clearly didn't hear her acid comment, "It would be a damn sight more unhealthy to be hit by a bomb," before he turned away to smile benignly at Mum and tweak a wide-eyed Jill under the chin.

"But we'll have to find somewhere to hide you from them German bombs won't we, little maid?" he told her.

Mum's instinct, as ever, was to pour oil on troubled waters. Before Gan could open her mouth again, she hastily asked the old man, "Where do you suggest, Mr Brown?"

She received an answer from both Gan and the warden at the same time.

Gan's was heavy with scorn. "If you think we're going to cram five of us into a glorified broom cupboard, you've got another think coming. Why, I'd sooner sit out in the wash-house!"

Unhearing, the kindly warden advised Mum, "Don't you try and get in that cupboard for a start. You'd be spiflicated." He opened the back door and peered through. "No, your best bet is this wash-house. It's at the back of the house and would be protected from blast by the high ground behind it."

Mum let him out of the front door. Gan was, very temporarily, lost for words.

Her luck was out when the vicar called. She had kept the Reverend Webster out of Millpool Head by always seeing him first on the several occasions he tried to call on us. This time, Mum answered the door while Gan was out in the wash-house. Mum hadn't the hard-faced confidence to keep him on the doorstep as Gan would have done, had she made the mistake of answering the door in the first place. By the time Gan had returned, the vicar was in, standing warming his back against the cooking range.

12

The Reverend Webster was a very tall, thin man, with an austere thin-lipped face. His head nearly reached one of the open ceiling beams above him as he stood, feet apart on our shabby hearth-rug. He had a curious way of not looking at any one of us, his contemplative gaze always on a point somewhere above our heads, or interestedly inspecting his own shoes.

Mum, struck dumb as she always was with strangers when in Gan's presence, picked up Jill to cuddle and left Gan to conduct a spirited dialogue with the vicar.

"I haven't seen you and your family at Church, Mrs Cooper," the Reverend Webster began.

Gan told him firmly, "We're not church-goers."

"I'm sorry to hear that. Don't you think we all have need of God in these troubled times?"

"God will look after us all, whether we go to church or not."

"But it is his wish that we should join together in prayer."

Gan asked bluntly, "How do you know that?"

The Reverend Webster sighed, fixing his eyes on a gently blowing cobweb which dangled from the beam near his head. "It is my mission to interpret the will of God," he said quietly. "Jesus used the analogy of the shepherd and his sheep. I am here to lead my parishioners to God."

Gan's colour had begun to heighten. "But we're not your sheep, Vicar. And I'm sorry, but I've got a pie in the oven." With that, she started to move purposefully towards the door.

The Reverend Webster's gaze dropped from the cobweb, sliding past Gan without stopping, to rest on his feet. He pointed his toe into a hole in the hearth-rug. "I regret your attitude, Mrs Cooper. I shall pray for you, that you may turn to God's love."

Gan said stiffly, "You pray for those as needs it. I can say my own prayers, thank you Vicar."

The hole in the rug was getting bigger beneath the vicar's exploring foot, though it was doubtful he even saw it. He sighed again, absent-mindedly flicked a floating strand of hessian from his shoe and moved with dignity towards the door.

He passed Mum, sitting with Jill on her knee, Diane and I hovering nervously behind her. Though he didn't appear to look at Jill, his hand unerringly found her head. He patted it in a benedictory fashion.

"You will, of course, be bringing this child to be christened?" he said to Mum, and she immediately started to flounder.

"Well, yes . . . that is . . . I don't . . ."

Gan settled it. "No," she said firmly. "The other two haven't been done and we believe in treating them all the same." And ignoring the Reverend Webster's horrified exclamation she flung open the door. "And now, if you don't mind . . ."

She closed the door with a sigh of relief. "For heaven's sake, let's have a cup of tea," she begged, a plea which became so familiar in the hardships and dangers to come, I still think of her whenever I brew up.

CHAPTER
THREE

'Put that light out!'
(*ARP Warning*)

1939 drew to a close. Nothing much had happened on the home front, but there had been a great deal of preparation for when it did.

Everyone agreed that Millbrook would not be in the front line, that Plymouth and Devonport would be the enemy's targets.

As the crow flies, Plymouth wasn't far away. You could stand in the hilly field behind our house and see the city lights across the narrow stretch of the Tamar. Until the blackout, that is.

The blackout was very strictly enforced, and anyone who inadvertently showed even a flicker of light was pounced on by neighbours, no less vigilant than the ARP warden. We didn't dare to be careless, with Warden Brown living opposite, his windows no more than ten feet from ours across the very narrow street.

Offences in the village were dealt with quickly and efficiently, either by a severe telling-off from PC Polworthy or a fatherly stricture from old Mr Brown. But people living in less insular areas were not treated so tolerantly.

Mrs Pendennis had a friend living in Plymouth who was prosecuted for showing a light. Meeting Gan in the meat queue, she poured an indignant tale into her old neighbour's ears.

"It's not right, Mrs Cooper. As if Hilda would do it deliberately, with four kids as well as her old man and her mother in the house. It stands to reason she was innocent, but she got fined £5."

"Well if she was innocent, she shouldn't be paying a fine." Gan's indignation matched Mrs Pendennis's. "Can't she appeal, insist she didn't show a light?"

"Oh no, Hilda would never perjury herself. She couldn't bring herself to do it." Both women shuffled forward with the queue.

"But . . . do you mean she did show a light?"

"Well yes, but it wasn't her fault. She thought you only had to black-out the windows at the front of the house. And fancy . . . Hilda's sure the magistrate didn't believe her!"

"Fancy," Gan said faintly. Reaching the counter, she passed over our ration books. "Stewing steak if you've got it, please."

"Sorry, I've only scrag end of mutton this week."

Before rationing, Gan had not been one of Mr Martin's regular customers. Rabbit from an unofficial supplier was more often than not the only meat we could afford.

Tight-lipped, she put the meat and ration books in her bag and was turning away just as the butcher gave Mrs Pendennis a conspiratorial wink.

"Bit of the usual, me dear," he murmured and passed her a packet already wrapped.

Mrs Pendennis was still carrying on about her friend Hilda. "I mean did he think she wanted a bomb to drop on her? Thank you ever so, Mr Martin." Her chins wobbled her gratitude. "My old man'll be tickled pink." She followed Gan out of the shop.

"I told her, our PC Polworthy would have believed her."

But Gan's equanimity had been too sorely tried. "Oh, I don't know," she said shortly. "PC Polworthy might be fair, but he's not daft."

That was the start of a cooling-off between her and Mrs Pendennis, which lasted until a row with Mrs Murdoch reunited them.

We had all been issued with gas masks, Jill being given a colourful red and blue one which brought a dismayed howl from her every time Mum tried to put her in it. And we all knew what kind of attack to expect, if we heard a rattle, a siren, or the church bells ringing.

A great deal of military traffic began to come through the village, to and from Tregantle Fort and the gun-sites along the cliffs. All of it edged past our house, to continue the difficult manoeuvre round the sharp bend into Dodbrook. We began to get used to seeing soldiers everywhere. Two or three of them were often crammed into our tiny living-room, being sustained with cups of tea or a glass of Gan's home-made elderberry wine, while their less fortunate colleagues cursed their way two inches forward, one back, past a worried Mrs Finchcombe's corner cottage.

But despite the general preparation for war, people were more concerned with local issues. The weather in the New Year was bitterly cold, the worst many remembered. Short of blankets, Mum and Gan piled everything they could find on our beds at night. It was not uncommon for poor families to use their overcoats as extra bedding. Diane and I, sharing a bed, had the bedside rag-rug thrown over us too, without Gan ever seeing the necessity for shaking it first.

An escape of convicts from Dartmoor caused general concern for many nervous villagers, to whom they posed a bigger threat than Hitler. We did not take a daily paper, so did not know of the break-out until Mrs Timble brought the news. Gan was pleased to see her, despite a sarcastic aside to me, the only one home with her since the others were out shopping, of "I suppose she's come to be nosey," before she opened the door.

Mrs Timble was the only neighbour at Millpool Head with whom Gan hadn't had a row. This was because Mrs Timble knew her place.

While not exactly obsequious, she agreed with all Gan's pronouncements, echoed all her opinions of the other neighbours, and though Gan had little respect for Mrs Timble, she needed a crony so visits were encouraged.

After an all-encompassing look round our shabby room, with sharp button-brown eyes which seemed to see every undusted corner, Mrs Timble came out with her news.

"Did you read the news about them convicts escaping?" she began importantly, knowing we would not have.

But she never got the better of Gan. Fetching the heavy brown tea-pot from the range, where it was in a perpetual state of brewing, Gan calmly set it down on the table and sent me to fetch a cup for our visitor. She took her time pouring out two cups of the dark, strong brew, before sitting down.

"I knew about it before it was in the papers," she said, grandly. "I saw it in the tea-leaves."

Mrs Timble's expression was a study, deflation fighting the healthy respect she held for Gan's tea-leaves readings. "Well fancy that, Mrs Cooper," she exclaimed. "What did you see?"

Gan took a satisfying gulp of tea. She relished it strong and sweet, never seeming to notice how others grimaced when they drank it. Lowering the cup from her lips she looked gravely at her visitor. "Trouble," she said. "Trouble and confusion. The cup was full of it."

"Oh. Well . . ." Mrs Timble hastened to make up for her rather lame response with a theatrical shiver. "Well, let's hope they catch the devils and put 'em back where they belong. They're more dangerous than animals, some of them Dartmoor convicts."

"It's to be hoped they do, for their own sakes. Poor blighters, they'll freeze to death on Dartmoor in this weather."

Mrs Timble instantly agreed. "Yes, poor souls. They're human beings after all."

Gan carefully drank, to leave the last dreg in her cup. "I'll do another reading if you like," she offered. Mrs Timble moved her chair closer, with flattering interest.

Gan swished the cup round three times, before turning it upside down onto her saucer. Then she carefully took it up into her cupped hands.

After closely scrutinising the spread of tea-leaves, from bottom to brim, she announced in an impressively slow voice, "I see more trouble, at the top of the cup now, so it's coming nearer. There's a dog at the bottom, that means treachery. And above the dog . . ." she twisted the cup sideways, ". . . is the number two."

Mrs Timble said diffidently, "I think there were three of them," but Gan ignored her.

"Whether the two means how many will be caught, or how many days they will be free, I can't tell. But the two is very significant."

I thought she had forgotten I was there, but she hadn't. "Betty, you shouldn't be listening," she reproved. "Take these cups to the wash-house, will you?"

Mum came in at that moment, with Diane and Jill, and Mrs Timble got up from the table, picking up her coat from the back of her chair.

"I was just telling your mother about the escaped convicts," she started to tell Mum.

Mum had no time to utter the startled question which had flashed across her face before Gan firmly interrupted, "You remember, Ida, I saw it in the tea-leaves." Whether Mum remembered or not, she knew better than to contradict.

I hurried Diane into the wash-house, where we pored over the cups. We couldn't see any dogs or numbers, no trouble, nothing but a collection of messy tea-leaves. Not for the first time, we were deeply impressed with Gan's uncanny gift.

CHAPTER
FOUR

'How to put out an incendiary bomb.'
(*ARP Leaflet*)

We began to get sporadic raids in the spring of 1940. They were hit and miss, causing little damage but a great deal of indignation. Villagers were up in arms when two cows were killed on an outlying farm, and we joined the trek of sightseers who toiled up Donkey Lane to inspect a crater in a field just below Whitsands.

These early raids aroused a degree of bravado in some of the more self-expressive village women. Mrs Dobson boasted to anyone who would listen, of what she would do to any Nazi who landed in Millbrook, and even Gan could not get a word in edgeways when Mrs Dobson was in full voice.

As that stout lady waddled down the street to catch Mrs Finchcombe coming out of the Co-op, Gan tartly observed, "That woman could talk the hind legs off Lord Haw-Haw," prudently waiting until Mrs Dobson was out of earshot before she said it.

The mood changed after the fall of France. News began to filter through of the evacuation at Dunkirk and solemn-faced women gathered in anxious little groups down the shopping end of West Street.

"I've heard they're bringing some of the soldiers back to Plymouth," Mrs Timble told everybody, and since her husband was a regular Petty Officer who had been away in the Navy since the outbreak of war, people thought she had inside knowledge.

"So we should see the ships in the Sound," said Gan. That afternoon we walked to Cawsand, an old fishing village two miles from Millbrook, overlooking Plymouth Sound.

We saw a breathtaking sight. The bay was filled with ships of all sorts and sizes, and some of the men had been landed at Cawsand. Tired, with blistered feet, they sat on the sea walls above the beach, and along the narrow, steeply rising lanes, their backs against the cottage walls. Villagers brought out cups of tea and sandwiches for them. Gan had brought the few cigarettes she and Mum had and handed them out to some of the men at her feet.

"Just what I've been dreaming about, Missus . . . a fag and Home Sweet Home," one grateful soldier thanked her, the weary grimace on his face the nearest he could get to a smile.

Raids began to get more frequent, with the enemy entrenched just across the English Channel. German bombers on their way to Plymouth flew over Millbrook, sometimes unloading an odd bomb they had got left on to us, on their way home. But our first really close shave in the summer of

1940 wasn't a bomb. And it happened so quickly, nobody had time to be frightened until it was all over.

We had heard the siren but had become accustomed to ignoring it, unless PC Polworthy came round blowing his whistle. That was the signal for raiders directly over us. With no whistle that day we stayed put.

The bus from Whitsands came past our house, cutting out the daylight from our small window. Out of nowhere came the high-pitched shriek of an aeroplane engine, and the staccato rattle of a machine-gun.

Stunned, we all stared at one another until Gan, recovering first, ordered, "Stay where you are," and dashed outside.

The plane was out of sight and so was the bus. With commendable presence of mind, the driver had swung his large vehicle round Dodbrook, instead of following his usual straight route down the main street. Unable to manoeuvre so quickly, the enemy pilot lost him and no one was hurt.

The bus driver was the village hero. Even Mrs Finchcombe, who had rushed to her window when she heard the attack and watched, aghast, as the bus lurched to within inches of her cottage, had recovered enough to sing his praises. She was invited round to our house that evening, to drink a fortifying glass of elderberry wine. Whether from that, or from the shared exhilaration of surviving danger, she, Mum and Gan spent a convivial hour, Diane and I listening

to their noisy laughter from our dark little bedroom upstairs.

This attack brought home to the villagers a sense of involvement with Plymouth which they had not previously felt. Before it, people had felt the rather complacent sympathy of the safe outsider for that vulnerable city. Now it was realised that, with Plymouth only five miles away as the bomber flies, the villages of this quiet, east Cornwall peninsula were not as far behind the front line as had been thought.

As well as high explosives, German raiders began to drop an increasing number of incendiary bombs. Though not as lethal as the HE's, they could cause enormous damage in old, close-knit streets, especially when nobody had seen where they fell. People were recruited as fire-watchers, to keep a lookout from some high, strategic place during night raids.

The Government began to issue a stream of directives, and people like Gan, who was intensely patriotic, followed them to the letter. We were instructed to clear lofts and attics, often the first seat of fire, and Mum struggled not too willingly, up a rickety ladder, at Gan's exhortations, to see what was in our attic.

A musty smell hit us, as soon as she lifted up the loft door, and Mum quailed. "There's nothing here, Mum," she called, but Gan was firm.

"You haven't looked properly," she said severely, and passed Mum a candle stuck in a saucer. Mum carefully took the candle and held it above her head to examine the attic.

We all heard the rustling noise which brought her stumbling down the ladder.

"There's a bird up there," she gasped.

When I remember it now, I realise that Gan had some grounds for her frequent accusations against me of showing off. Because that is exactly what I did. Though just as terrified as the others of a wildly fluttering bird in that dark and eerie place, I volunteered to go up and let it out through the skylight.

The bird was too frightened to approach while I was pushing up the window latch, but when I had retreated back to the ladder, after a hasty glance round the otherwise empty loft, I saw it flutter out, a blackbird with a bright yellow beak. I returned to secure the window, picked up the flickering candle and made my trembling way down the ladder.

My heart was racing and my hands were sticky with sweat. But even though I was only nine I must have hidden the effort my bravado had cost me beneath an irritating mask of nonchalance, because nobody praised me.

We had another visit from the ARP warden, this time to tell us how to put out incendiary bombs. To Gan's annoyance, he called just as she was on the point of ladling out our regular Monday bubble-and-squeak dinner from the frying pan.

He gave us a leaflet on how to put out incendiary bombs, then proceeded to read a copy of it out loud, despite Gan's exasperated attempts to cut him short, so that she could get back to her frying pan.

"Have a bucket always ready, filled with sand or earth," he read, then looked up and added, "You can buy this special stuff to squirt on the bombs, Mrs Cooper, but take my word for it, a good dollop of wet earth is just as good."

"Yes, we've already . . ." Gan began, but Mr Brown's eyes had already returned to his leaflet.

"Make sure all members of the family know where it is," he read, before earnestly adjuring her, "But mind you don't leave it where somebody can fall over it, me dear. There've been one or two nasty accidents with fire buckets."

"It's in the wash-house, well out of the way." Gan then tried dropping a strong hint, "Ida, go and see if the dinner's burning," but she didn't get that bit out before Mr Brown had looked away.

"You have to act quickly, not give it a chance to take hold," he warned. "And don't you worry." He peered under the rim of his tin-hat. "If I sees one drop on you when I'm out on my warden duties, I'll be here like a shot, seeing as you've no man," and there was enough kindness in his short-sighted eyes to freeze the tart words on Gan's lips.

"That's very kind of you," she said gruffly. "Thank you, Mr Brown."

Gan always preferred men to women, despite, or perhaps because of, our being an entirely female family. Several of the friendships she made with women were mainly due to a patriotic loyalty to their absent men.

Mrs Timble was partly tolerated because her husband was fighting in the Navy. Mrs Finchcombe had a son at sea and Gan never refused her the chance to talk about Billy as a boy, no matter how much she might explode into exasperation after Mrs Finchcombe had gone.

Our new next-door neighbours were a young couple with a little boy of four. Greg Hawkins was a big, fair-haired man, ruddy-complexioned and his son was a miniature copy of him. But his wife was a pretty little red-head, with large, appealing blue eyes in a sweetly innocent face. Greg worked at the brickworks at Southdown, but he was also known to us as a supplier of rabbits at sixpence each.

We had first got to hear of Greg's little sideline from Mrs Timble, who had earnestly enjoined Gan, "Don't tell anyone else though. He keeps it on the quiet." But since Gan later got the same information from Mrs Finchcombe and old Mrs Brown, he had obviously not kept it quiet enough.

It seemed as though our source of cheap meat was going to dry up that summer, however, for Greg got his calling-up papers. After going on a small-arms course in Devon, he came home on embarkation leave, loftily superior about his fellow recruits' lack of success with a gun.

"Some of 'em couldn't hit an elephant at ten feet," he scornfully told Mum and Gan, when he came to say goodbye.

Greg had a request to make. "Keep an eye on Tilda for me while I'm away, Mrs Cooper," he asked gruffly. "If she needs someone to turn to, you'll be here, won't you?"

Keeping an eye on Tilda must have seemed a simple promise to make. Gan willingly gave it, without an inkling of the dance that biddable young woman would lead her.

CHAPTER
FIVE

'Penalty for listening in to a foreign
radio station — Penal Servitude or Death.'
(*Emergency Legislation*)

Diane and I went to the Church of England school at the top of Blindwell Hill. Infants were taken there but after the age of seven the school was for girls only. Boys were sent a couple of miles in the opposite direction, to Four Lanes End.

Right from the beginning of the war, schoolchildren were closely involved. We stood, packed together in the hall, the Monday after Chamberlain's speech, listening to Miss Swithin, the Headmistress, telling us we must all pray, so that we would win the war.

Whenever I hear the hymn we sang that day, *Oh God our Help in Ages Past*, I still remember the awe I felt, a sense of dangers to come without any understanding of what they would be.

The next day the vicar came to take our assembly and told us we must pray for our enemies as well as ourselves. Gan exploded when we told her. "Don't you dare!" she fiercely forbade us. "Let the Germans say their own prayers."

We immediately started having Air Raid Practices. There were no school shelters. At the ringing of the school bell, we were taken out in orderly lines by our teachers, to hide in the tall hedgerows further up Blindwell Hill. Mrs Steel, one of the infant teachers, dashed up and down the lane, shoving us further into the dense leaves if we so much as exposed an arm or a leg, exhorting us not to turn our faces up to the sky in case an enemy raider saw us, until Miss Swithin told her to get herself into the hedges with us.

As the winter drew in, we got real air-raids and we began to shelter in the cellars beneath the school. With no perception of the risk, we all wanted to sit round the huge boiler which heated the school, and were filled with disappointment when another class got there first.

It was at school that Diane and I became aware of our poverty. We were too young to feel any stigma at being offered free school meals, in a letter from my teacher, but Gan and Mum felt it.

"That woman's got a cheek," was Gan's indignant response. "Does she think we can't feed our own children?" Mum gave me a politely written refusal to take back to school. So we continued to come home for what was invariably bread dipped in Oxo or cream-cracker sandwiches, and never felt deprived.

Real humiliation came when we had to strip to pants and vest for PT and found that other girls had real vests, not old jumpers from which the sleeves had been cut.

It would not have been quite so bad if the sleeves had been picked out, instead of being hacked off in Gan's rough and ready fashion. The girl next to me pulled at the loose strand of wool from my dark green garment, her intrigued giggle as it unravelled in her hand deeply hurting me.

Diane suffered the added ignominy of her vest having the distinctive 'vee' neck, purple edged on grey, of what had obviously been a boy's pullover. It was a typical example of Gan's domination over her daughter as well as us, that Mum wouldn't have dared to suggest a little more finesse in the way the old woollens, bought as a bundle from a second-hand clothes shop in Devonport, could be adapted. It would never have occurred to Diane and me to complain.

Gan suffered a humiliation herself regarding clothes, but her response was characteristically more robust than our silent suffering. She sallied forth in a brown and white striped dress, bought from the Devonport shop, and was hailed from across West Street by Mrs

Dobson, the rag-and-bone man's lady, who was wearing a larger version of the same dress.

Mrs Dobson was hugely delighted. "Well, where did you get yours?" she called to Gan. "I got mine off my old man's Friday collection."

Instantly Gan exclaimed, "Would you believe it! And to think that woman in the dress shop had the nerve to tell me this was an exclusive model. That's the last time I shall shop there." For that reason, and others which arose later, we never patronised Mrs Reuben's of Devonport again.

Gan's attitude to our teachers in general was one of reluctant respect, until one of them sent a message home. Other women shared this prejudice, that the school did its job, parents did theirs, and never the twain should meet. Mrs Dewey, mother of a naughty infant boy, clearly expressed village opinion when she received a note containing helpful advice from Mrs Steel and indignantly declared, "They can learn our Eric if they want to, but they're not going to learn me."

Pupils in Diane's class were given notes to bring home, asking parents not to allow their children to listen to Lord Haw-Haw.

Gan was disgusted. "They must think we're daft, if they think we'd let you listen to that drivel." We knew that she and Mum listened in that first year of war, to the propaganda broadcasts from Germany.

Diane said, "Mary Penhallow's mother lets her stay up to listen."

"Well, Mary Penhallow's mother wants her head looking into." It almost seemed as though Gan, in her self-righteousness, had accepted the school letter as justified.

But Diane's next words changed her mind. That incurably honest child said, "Miss Vickerstaff thinks it's terrible. She says people are breaking the law when they listen to Lord Haw-Haw."

Gan went stiff, from her neck down to her black-laced shoes. "Well, you can tell Miss Vickerstaff . . ." Out came the familiar command, hurled at us whenever we passed on something from school which did not meet with her approval. "You can tell Miss Vickerstaff from me that this is a free country, that's what we're fighting for, and if we want to listen to Lord Haw-Haw we will."

Poor Diane was suitably squashed, while I basked in the unfamiliar role for once, of not being in the wrong.

Around this time I began to tell lies. They did not seem like lies at first, just the development of my fertile imagination. It went berserk after one of the earlier raids while we were at school and I went home afterwards and told Mum and Gan a real whopper.

We had seen planes in the sky, their vapour trails making interconnecting circles above the creek, as our teachers hurried us down to the cellars. The raid did not last long. We barely had time to eat the emergency snack we all carried in our gas-mask boxes, which was supposed to be for if we got trapped but which we all looked on as an air-raid perk, before the All-Clear sounded.

I had no thought of the tale I would tell as I hurried home down Blindwell Hill with Diane; it certainly was not planned. But the sight of Mum and Gans' anxious faces, as they waited at the door for us, had an exhilarating effect on me. The exciting story sprang out of my mouth, almost before I had time to invent it.

I hung up my gas-mask behind the door and announced importantly, "We saw a German plane shot down at school today."

"What?" A gasp burst from both Mum and Gan. I was the centre of attention.

"It was shot down by one of ours and came whizzing down, with flames pouring out of it."

37

Mum and Gan exchanged horrified glances. "Did it land near the school?" Mum looked really shaken.

"Yes, in one of the fields near our playground. A man with a parachute jumped out of it."

By this time, Diane was as spellbound as Mum and Gan. "I never saw anything," she confessed, her eyes round with disappointment. "Miss Vickerstaff told us to hurry, and not to look up."

Gan demanded, "Are you telling me you were outside when this happened?"

"Yes, we were on our way to the cellars. The siren had just gone, and we . . ."

"Well, you damn well shouldn't have been." Gan looked angrily at Mum. "I think we should have a word with the school, Ida. They should have kept the children under cover until the planes had passed over."

I began to see my moment of glory disappearing under Gan's inherent inclination to blame the school for any and everything, and rushed into a fatal error.

"Then we saw some men jump out from behind a hedge and capture him," I gabbled. "They all had guns and they marched him away with his hands up."

There was a deathly silence, before Gan shouted at me, "You've made all this up, you little devil. Get upstairs!"

As I shot up the stairs before Gan could get near enough to wallop me, I heard her exclaim to Mum, "I *thought* that damned tale was too far-fetched to be true!"

That's what she thought. By a strange twist of irony, my highly embellished story of the enemy raider was to pale into insignificance, compared with the near farcical events when one did come down near the village, less than a month later.

CHAPTER
SIX

'Dig for Victory.'
(*Government Poster*)

Our teachers gradually began to organise ways in which children could help the war effort. Miss Croft made herself responsible for salvage and got the entire school enthusiastically collecting newspapers and bringing them to the house at the bottom of Blindwell Hill where she lived alone. Before the war was a year old, she had a room perpetually stacked high with newspapers. As fast as it was collected, we took her some more.

We were all given knitting lessons, Miss Vickerstaff in particular inspiring us with vivid descriptions of air-gunners in their freezing cold aeroplanes, longing for mittens to warm their hands, and merchant seamen on sea-soaked decks, desperate for balaclavas. Piles of wool were put in front of us, Air Force blue and thick, oiled white, and I couldn't wait to get started on it.

I had become a very good knitter by the time I was ten, but Diane always hated it, never getting beyond the finger-shaping of her poor air-gunner's mittens.

Miss Croft's particular interest was refugees, and she had us knitting squares, forty-eight stitches wide, forty-eight rows long, to make up into blankets. I remember her aesthetic desire for balance coming into conflict with Gan's practical desire to save work, when Gan insisted I knitted all the squares I did at home in one long strip.

"What's the sense in casting them all off just to sew them together again?" she demanded, and I never had the nerve to tell her that Miss Croft stitched over the knitted joins, so they would match the rest.

Miss Swithin and the older girls dug up part of the grassed section of our playground, and planted potatoes, selling them for the Spitfire Fund. For quite a long time Gan, always willing to help the war effort, gave me money to buy them. I went so often to the Headmistress's room after school, where she kept boxes of potatoes under her desk, a set of heavy scales alongside, that though normally a rather forbidding figure to me, she became more approachable.

I actually began to talk to her, something I rarely did with anyone outside the family. Then, as I passed messages between her and Gan, things began to go wrong.

"Your family eat a lot of potatoes, Betty," Miss Swithin remarked one day. "Ask your mother if she would like a leaflet on different ways to cook them. They're tuppence each for the Spitfire Fund."

Giving the potatoes to Gan I said, "Miss Swithin says would you like to know how to cook them?"

She instantly bridled. "What have you been saying to her?" she demanded and I hastily denied having said anything.

I was too young to realise that Miss Swithin's well-meaning offer, or the way I relayed it, had hit Gan below the belt. She hated cooking and never had the patience to take trouble with it. Potatoes in our house were never properly drained and never, ever mashed, just a watery lumpy mass heaped onto our plates with the admonition, if anyone looked askance, "Get it eaten or go without!"

She never needed to say that to me, since I was always hungry enough to eat anything, but Diane had slightly more refined taste-buds than I had. She was frequently the target of Gan's wrath at the table.

But I understood I must choose my words more carefully. "Gan said to thank you very much," I effusively assured Miss Swithin. "But she knows how to cook potatoes, so she doesn't need a leaflet."

"Oh but . . ." Miss Swithin straightened up from the box under her desk and finished good-naturedly, "That's all right then, Betty." She weighed out half a stone and put them in my bag. "I hope your grandmother saves all her peelings for the pig-swill bin," she smiled, giving me threepence change. "The pigs need all they can get."

I said to Gan, "Miss Swithin says she hopes you give the pigs our peelings," and was promptly told:

"Well, she's got another hope coming. You can tell her . . ." I felt a quake of alarm at the familiar prelude to a falling-out. "We use our potato peelings on the fire, to save fuel for the war effort."

"Gan thinks it's better to throw our peelings on the fire," I told Miss Swithin, and immediately sensed a slight withdrawal in her manner. I tried to make amends.

"We put all sorts on our fire. We go out collecting wood and the other day Diane picked up what she thought was a knobby bit but when Mum emptied the bag when we got home, it was a bit of dog dirt." I rattled out what I thought was a very funny tale and drew a kindly glance from Miss Swithin.

"Actually, burning animal excreta is not so strange in these times of shortage, Betty," she told me. "I believe some of the farmers are now burning sheep manure to save fuel."

"Do you know what Miss Swithin said?" I exclaimed, as soon as I got home. I thought the information fascinating. "She says you could burn manure."

Gan exploded. I thought she was going to hit me, and instinctively leapt back out of her reach. "Manure? What the devil does she take us for? Does she think we're that hard up?"

"No, she only . . ." I began to quaver but Gan wouldn't listen.

"You tell her from me, if she thinks it's such a good idea, she can put it on her own fire."

That was the last time she let me buy potatoes from school, so my friendly little chats with the Headmistress came to an abrupt halt. I was glad really. Adapting her and Gans' messages to make them more acceptable to each other had become quite a strain.

Although Gan's attitude to any advice handed out by our teachers was that of the bull to the red rag, it was a different matter when PC Polworthy came to the school to caution us. Parents encouraged their children to have a healthy respect for the village policeman, and Gan was no exception. Everything he said to us, she wholeheartedly endorsed.

Very early in the war all signposts had been taken down, and the name Millbrook painted out above the Co-op window.

"Do you know why we have done that?" PC Polworthy wanted to know and the hands of a hundred and fifty children shot up, all wanting to tell him it was so that the Germans would get lost if they invaded us.

"Very good," PC Polworthy beamed at us. "So what would you do if a stranger asked you the way to somewhere?"

"We wouldn't tell him."

"We'd tell 'im the wrong way."

"I'd fetch our Dad."

"Dan and I would kick 'im in the . . ."

"Scream," screamed Effie Dewey.

Excited responses burst from the children, so that Miss Swithin had to restore order.

"Don't be so rude," she reproved us. "One at a time. Johnny Penhallow." She pointed at an infant bouncing up and down in the front row.

"Run and tell a policeman," he said importantly.

"Very good." PC Polworthy stepped forward to pat Johnny on the head. "But first and foremost, *don't tell them where to go*. Not even . . ." and he cast a stern eye around the hall, "Not even if you are offered money or sweets."

In the thoughtful silence that followed, Johnny Penhallow's treble voice piped up. "Not even cake?"

"No, not even cake."

"Not even a biscuit?"

The policeman's prominent blue eyes rolled towards Miss Swithin, who said, severely, "Johnny, you are not to take anything from anybody. Is that clear?" With a vigorous nodding of his black-curled head, Johnny subsided back onto his bottom, on the wooden tiled floor.

"And now onto something else," said PC Polworthy. "The enemy have been dropping other things besides bombs. In some parts of Cornwall people have found leaflets from Hitler, trying to pretend he is our friend. We all know that isn't true, don't we?"

"Yeeeeees." The children's enthusiastic response was a crescendo in reverse, each child's voice fading away as he or she became aware of Miss Swithin's stern eye on them.

"I shall not warn you again," she spoke quietly as the lull fell, and she didn't need to. We all knew we had gone too far.

"Any leaflets you find are to be brought straight to your teachers, or to me. But if you should see any packages or parcels, anything strange lying around in the fields or hedges, leave them alone and tell a grown-up."

PC Polworthy paused and looked at us very seriously. "They could be what we call booby-traps. That is, small bombs that will hurt anyone who picks them up. Don't touch *anything* suspicious."

He had us spellbound, from the top girls to the newest infant. And when we poured it all out to Mum and Gan, when we got home, they were just as impressed.

"Make sure you do everything the policeman says," Gan warned us. "If I catch either of you accepting sweets or picking up booby-traps, I'll wring your necks."

What with her and the policeman, we became totally brainwashed.

Diane adamantly refused to direct a woman who had just got off the Whitsands bus, to the Co-op at the end of West Street. And we were both horrified when Effie Dewey's Grandad, whom we had known for two years, proffered a bag of liquorice allsorts as we passed him, leaning over the bottom half of the stable door of his whitewashed cottage.

"There you are, take one, little maids," he smiled, and we fled full tilt down Blindwell Hill, convinced that the kind old man had been recruited by the German Secret Service.

A few days after his visit to our school, Gan's respect for our representative of Law and Order was severely tested. She fell foul of PC Polworthy when, during a daylight raid in which he had already blown his whistle warning of raiders overhead, he saw Gan outside in the street, peering up at the enemy planes on their way to Plymouth.

"Get under cover, woman," he shouted at her and she scurried in. She must have seen my astonished expression, at her having taken a telling-off without giving a mouthful back. Her face flamed but for once, I was too slow to take warning.

"And you get away from that window." She took her discomfiture out on me and yanked me painfully away by my ear. "Didn't you hear that whistle? Do as the policeman says and take cover."

CHAPTER
SEVEN

'It's one of ours, chasing one of theirs.'
(*Gan*)

As the raids of autumn 1940 got heavier and nearer to home, Gan employed all sorts of devices to bolster our courage.

Some were the same as everybody else's. She taught us to recognise the different sound of the enemy planes from ours, her hearing apparently so acute that she could distinguish the steady drone of one of ours, chasing one of theirs. And at the end of the raid, when German bombers flew away from Plymouth, over us to the open sea, she could even count their throbbing engines and claim there were fewer of them going home.

She encouraged us to listen for our own ack-ack guns, firing from sites all around us, the sentinels to Plymouth Sound. Their characteristic 'Pip-pip, boom-boom' became reassurance to us that we were fighting back.

But one ploy Gan used was distinctly weird, though at the time we all, even my mother so far as I knew, accepted it without question. When I think about it now, I can hardly believe my own credulity, even though I was only nine.

Mum and Gan enjoyed reading, and in particular books by Baroness Orczy about the 'Scarlet Pimpernel'. Gan began to imbue this fictitious character whose real identity was supposed to be Sir Percy Blakeney, with the power to influence us from the spirit world.

The Scarlet Pimpernel had a League in these books, a band of followers, all brave and true. Gan wrote out a list of these characters and began adding other names to theirs. Anyone who had done something heroic was written in her little red book.

Some of them were heroes of the First World War. Two names I remember were Earl Jellicoe and Albert Ball, a Nottingham VC.

It made no difference to Gan whether they were alive or dead. Air aces of the Battle of Britain were frequently in the news. Paddy Finucane, Cobber Kane, Guy Gibson, John Cunningham; Gan enrolled them all as members of the League of the Scarlet Pimpernel. She put us in as honorary members and Sir Percy became the custodian of our courage. Any sign of fear and we had him reproaching us, via Gan.

The first time I remember being got out of bed was in a bad night raid on Plymouth, the first of the big incendiary attacks. Diane and I, burrowed like dormice beneath the heavy rag-rug, heard nothing of it until we were wakened by Gan shaking us.

The noise was deafening. Wave after wave of aircraft flew over us, hounded by the noisy barrage of guns from the sites above the village. On top of it all, PC Polworthy's whistle shrilled its warning, as he hurried down the street wearing his tin hat, from his home next to the police station, twenty yards up the road.

"Get dressed quickly," Gan ordered. Leaving me to dress myself, she struggled to push a bewildered Diane into a jumper and skirt.

Mum was lifting Jill, still fast asleep, out of her cot and wrapping her in a blanket, while Gan, Diane and I blundered around in the dark bedroom.

Through the window, above the hill behind the house, we could see flashes of gunfire and the thin, hunting blade of a solitary searchlight. We all stumbled downstairs to the wash-house, to huddle together on a wooden bench against the safer outer wall.

If any of us had thought about being frightened, we soon changed our minds. Three-year-old Jill was cuddled inside Mum's thick cardigan, her ears muffled from the noise. But Diane was taken to task, when Gan saw her trembling lip, in the flickering glow of a candle left ready on the boiler.

"Don't let Sir Percy see you cry," she said sternly. By the time she had turned her attention to me I had got a suitably stoical expression on my face. I was more afraid of Gan and Sir Percy than the bombs.

Gan did her usual count of returning planes. She had got to twenty-seven when Jill, waking to struggle out of the suffocating haven of Mum's cardigan, broke into a startled yell at the din suddenly hitting her ears. Mum got the blame for it.

"Now I've lost count," Gan reproached her. Mum got up, to walk round the boiler and back with Jill, making a not too successful attempt to sing 'Rock-a-Bye Baby' louder than the German bombers' intermittent drone.

Gan finally announced with her usual authority, "I reckon they've shot down at least a dozen. That's a few less to come here again."

It was as well we, and she, did not know how fallible she was.

A hundred planes had rained thousands of fire bombs on Plymouth that night, but that raid was nothing to the ones still to come.

The following morning, Diane and I got ready for school as usual, despite having been up half the night.

Gan doled out plates of her own special porridge recipe. It was thick and lumpy, and since she scraped out the pan down to the last lump, some of it often had a burnt flavour. But she sprinkled it with sugar, tipped some milk over it and ordered, "Get that down you and hurry up." So we did.

While we were eating, she went next door to see how Tilda Hawkins had fared during the raid. "If I'd thought, I'd have asked her to come round to us," she fretted.

She returned as we were putting on our waterproof capes, with their attached pixie hoods, and Diane was looking for her gas-mask.

"That little Tilda Hawkins has more guts than I'd have given her credit for," Gan said to Mum. "She says she wouldn't dream of letting Hitler drive her out of her own home. I told her, Greg would be proud of her. What have you lost?" This was an irritable aside to Diane.

"My gas-mask. I put it . . ."

"Wherever you put it, it's still there. Go and look in the wash-house. And hurry, or you'll be late for school."

Mum was dressing a fretful Jill. "Poor little mite, I think you need another sleep," she soothed. "Has Tilda heard from Greg?" she asked Gan.

"Yes, she says a lot of his letter was censored but something he wrote made her think he's somewhere hot. Anyway, some good news, Ida. One of Greg's workmates down at Southdown has taken over his rabbit shoot, till he comes home. Tilda says we can still have them for 6d each. It seems that George Dorman came round last night to see if she was all right, and that was when he offered. I'd have thought he was a bit old to go out rabbit shooting, but we'll see."

Mum said thoughtfully, "It might be the young George Dorman who's going out rabbit shooting. He would be the same age as Greg."

Diane had come back with her gas-mask and we stood waiting for Mum's goodbye kiss. Even we could not miss the sudden, frigid silence, before Gan said slowly, "Young George Dorman? But he's not a fire-watcher is he? That would be his father who came round to see Tilda last night."

"No. The father is in the Home Guard. Young George does fire-watching at night and works at the Southdown ropeworks during the day."

"Well, why wasn't he called up like Greg?" demanded Gan.

"I believe he was medically unfit . . ."

"Medically unfit!" Gan's tone was grim enough to strike a chill of alarm in Diane and me. With one accord, we sidled out through the door, foregoing Mum's kiss. We heard Gan's incomprehensible threat as we quietly closed the door behind us. "I'll give him medically unfit if he tries to do the dirty on Greg!"

We had no idea what she was talking about, and had more sense than to stay to find out.

Gan's preoccupation with the psychic extended far beyond the tea-leaves, a crystal ball which she had acquired before the war, and Sir Percy. She and Mum went to a Spiritualist Church in Devonport as often as they could afford the fare across the river on the *Western Belle*.

Sometimes Gan just took me, but often we all went, to sit on hard seats at the back of a room in some private house, full to the door with mostly women.

There was always a part of the service when a medium would go into a kind of trance, then announce she had made contact with someone on the other side.

On one occasion the woman said, "I have someone here who is surrounded by water." Not surprisingly, just about everyone in the room shot upright in their chairs.

The medium went on, "It is a man and now the water is behind him." She paused. "He has a message for someone in this room."

The atmosphere was tense. "Who is Charlie?" the woman suddenly asked, and Gan spoke up. It was the first time I ever heard her voice tremble. "My husband was Charlie," she said.

The medium spoke very kindly. "Well, Charlie has a message for you, my dear. He says, 'Keep your pecker up'." She closed her eyes for a few seconds before opening them to say, "He says to tell you, 'at least it was clean, my dear'. Does that mean anything to you?"

"Oh yes. Yes, it does." Diane and I, sitting next to each other, exchanged glances, though we were more impressed by Gan's display of emotion than the message, which meant nothing to us.

"He, my husband, was very fastidious. He hated to be dirty."

The medium nodded. "That's how I see him. And the water behind him, that was the sea, wasn't it?"

"Yes. Yes, it was."

"Well, remember his message to you my dear, and take heart, and now . . ." Her eyes closed again. "As he fades away, I am getting someone else. It is a woman, who sits in a chair, rocking to and fro."

She delivered messages to perhaps half-a-dozen eager women, before bringing the service to a close, with a hymn and a prayer.

"That was your Grandad," Gan told us when we got home. We knew Grandad had been killed in the First World War. "It was in Mesopotamia. We heard that many of our men were pushed back into the sea."

She sat quietly at the table, while Mum got the tea ready. Then she fetched her book of the League of the Scarlet Pimpernel, and added Grandad's name to it.

CHAPTER
EIGHT

'Watch out for impostors giving false orders.
They could be Germans in disguise.'
(*If the Invader Comes: Gov't. Pamphlet 1940*)

On the whole, Mum and Gan did not attempt to hide war news from Diane and me. Gan had a very robust attitude. "They might as well know what's going on," she insisted, and of course Mum agreed with her. It meant, certainly for me, a feeling of deep involvement. I remember sharing in Mum and Gan's pride at the Royal Navy's rescue of the *Altmark* sailors, and their indignation over the bombing of Coventry.

We knew about the possibility of invasion too. The Government had sent out leaflets after Dunkirk, telling people what to do.

We got one, entitled 'If the Invader Comes' and Diane and I picked up snippets of it, some of it passed on to us by Gan, but even more was overheard when she and Mum were discussing it.

"If the Germans land, we've all got to stay put," Gan told us. "Wherever you are, stay there."

"But, w . . . what if w . . . w . . . we're at s . . . s . . . school?" I stuttered. It wasn't that I really understood the enormity of the threat facing us, simply that I had developed a stutter. My teacher had written to Mum, suggesting it was caused by anxiety, Gan insisted it was merely attention seeking, while I knew it was simply due to my haste to get my words out before Gan shut me up.

"You . . . *stay* . . . there." Gan did not accept Miss Croft's advice, that I should be encouraged to speak more slowly, but evidently thought it would help if *she* did.

Mum said kindly, "They won't land, Betty. Our sailors won't let them."

"But we've all got to be brave," said Gan. "Remember who you are." Mum looked as confused as Diane and me, until Gan sharply reminded us all, "You are members of the League."

I was bursting with questions. "But if they d . . . did land here, if they got p . . . past the sailors, we could . . . could go to Auntie Lizzie's, could . . . couldn't we? She d . . . d . . ." But Gan's patience, always short, was at an end.

"No, we will not go to your Auntie Lizzie's," she said sharply. "We will stay here and face the Germans like everyone else. Go and get your coats, we're going up to Whitsands!"

Gan was part of a large family. She had managed to fall out with every member of it in turn, most of them still living in or near Nottingham, where she had been born. She had two sisters and three brothers, her eldest brother, John, having been killed in the First World War.

She was never on good terms with both of her sisters at the same time. We knew that she and Auntie Ida had fallen-out through the post, but hadn't caught up with their reconciliation over a row with Auntie Lizzie. At that time, we children had not met any of them.

We got a bag each, since we never walked the lanes without collecting wood. Jill was put into the push-chair and we set off.

As we passed the police station, PC Polworthy came out and called us a cheerful greeting. Gan had long forgiven him for shouting at her when he caught her plane-spotting. He grinned. "Are you going up to the cliffs? Mind you come and tell me if you see any Germans dressed up as British officers." He went on his way, chuckling.

"G . . . Germans? Dressing up? Wh . . . wh . . . ?" I was off again.

"It's just something in the Government leaflet," Gan said testily. "It's only if the Germans land, and they're not going to. Let's have no more about it. Come on, we'll go this way."

She evidently thought our courage needed testing. To Diane's, my and, I suspect Mum's dismay — Jill had not reached the age of anticipation — she chose, out of several different routes up to the cliffs, the one which lay past Wiggle Farm and an extremely belligerent flock of geese.

At the sight of Diane's trembling bottom lip, Mum attempted a half-hearted suggestion that we take the Donkey Lane route, but it had no effect. "If Hitler's not going to beat us, I'm damned if we're going to let a few geese," Gan insisted, and we followed her towards Wiggle Farm, like lambs to the slaughter.

As usual, the geese heard us coming. As we rounded the corner of the high-hedged lane, to come upon the large, open barnyard in front of Wiggle Farm, they rushed out to meet us, their necks stretched forward in unmistakable hostility, all those baleful beaks heading straight for us. How we ever got through them without being nipped I can't think, but we always did. We each had our own method of facing them.

Jill, her eyes popping with alarm over the cot blanket wrapped around her, shrank back into her push-chair as Mum propelled it past the front runners of the angry flock. Diane clung to the push-chair handle farthest away from the geese, her short legs batting to and fro like little pistons as she struggled to keep up with Mum.

Gan and I always brought up the rear. Every time we passed that farm she loudly exhorted everyone not to run, that it would only excite the geese. And every time, nobody took any notice but me.

I never had any choice. Gan was determined not to be intimidated and she insisted on having an ally. So while I wanted to run with the push-chair, instead I walked sedately beside Gan in apparent nonchalance. But I was fully aware that whereas the geese obviously knew Gan was not afraid of them, they knew I was.

A huge white monster hissed its contempt at my outwardly unwavering, inwardly petrified heels, until Gan grabbed at my pixie-hood and yanked me towards her in exasperation.

"For heaven's sake, I didn't say encourage them," she snapped. "Do you always have to show off?"

After Diane and I had gone to bed that night, we heard a knock on the front door. "Who do you think it is?" whispered Diane.

Creeping out of bed, I heard Mrs Timble's rather high-pitched voice through the half-open door at the bottom of the stairs.

Gan was inviting her to come in for a cup of tea. "I can't stop, I've left the kids," Mrs Timble protested but she still came in.

As I began to tiptoe back to bed, carefully avoiding a known creaking floorboard, I heard her say dramatically, "Well, what do you think about the latest then? If we run away when the Germans invade, they will machine-gun us."

I stopped, frozen, till I heard Gan's reassuringly scornful voice. "Chance'll be a fine thing," she snorted. "Let 'em get across the Channel first."

The concept of the English Channel as a defensive moat was very strong in people who lived along the south coast. Gan was no exception. There had been several rumours of submarines sighted in Whitsands Bay and she began to concentrate our walks along the cliffs, taking us to stare out over the barbed-wire beach across a choppy sea, as far out as Eddystone Lighthouse. She told us about a broadcast which Winston Churchill had made, giving us her own interpretation of it.

"He wants us all to be watchful, so that the Germans won't be able to land without us knowing. So we're going to do some submarine watching. See if you can see a periscope."

We would never have been able to pick one out, in that turbulent grey sea, but we felt as though we were helping to win the war. I did once ask, "What shall we do if we see a periscope?" but Gan looked at me as though she doubted my intelligence.

"Well what do you think?" she snapped. "Go and tell the policeman, of course."

Gan's refusal to tolerate any suggestion of cowardice, certainly from Diane and me, extended to physical pain. Like many of the schoolchildren, despite repeated warnings not to run down the very steep Blindwell Hill, we did it, and our knees suffered for it. Even worse injuries were got on the school path, which was covered in gravel. Time and again, one or the other of us went home with badly grazed knees and hands, and some of these wounds began to turn septic.

Gan's remedy for this was rough and ready in the extreme. She put a pad of cotton wool between a piece of old sheeting and soaked it in boiling water, before pressing it on our wound, to 'Kill the germs'. It was agonising and far worse than the pain of the original tumble. But we learned to bear it stoically, our tears not allowed to fall from our eyes because Gan and Sir Percy expressly forbade it.

It meant we grew up never expecting sympathy when we were hurt, and seeking always to hide our feelings from others. Gan was the only extrovert in our family. The rest of us built up a wall of reserve around ourselves, even between us and Mum, which was not bridged until Diane and I were young women.

Gan did have another, more light-hearted way in which she sought to keep her own and everybody else's pecker up. When she was not actually at odds with anyone or anything, she sang, loudly and all over the house. She had a good, strong voice and had been an enthusiastic visitor to the Victorian Music Halls when she was a girl. She knew all their songs and also the songs of the First World War. Added to the new war songs, she had a considerable repertoire.

She never really wanted us to accompany her, with one specific exception. I had a natural desire to sing, but my attempts to join in were as often as not greeted with an exasperated, "For heaven's sake, shut up Betty!" Not surprisingly, this would cut off my rendering of 'Oh, I do like to be . . . ' before I had even got to 'beside the seaside'. A quelling look from her, if we happened to be in eye contact, was enough to stifle my first note before I could utter it.

The exception was during air-raids, when we were all encouraged to sing, even Mum, who never really wanted to. In those cold autumn nights of 1940, Diane and I would huddle together on the rolled-up hearth-rug, grabbed up on our way to the wash-house, to lean against Mum's knee as she sat on the bench with Jill on her lap, Gan beside her, and sing.

We Packed up our Troubles in our old Kit-bags, Kept the Home Fires Burning, and exhorted the rabbits to Run, Run, Run, not quite drowning out the sounds of war above us, but certainly diluting it.

In intermittent lulls Gan would introduce a little variety with *Why am I always the Bridesmaid*, or perhaps the song of the Great Big Sword getting nearer to poor Little Vera. But as the bombers swarmed back from Plymouth, meeting the same noisy reception from the coastal ack-ack guns which they had met on the way in, it was back to patriotism and a spirited rendering of *There'll Always be an England*.

The next day, it would be back to normal. Woe betide me if I momentarily forgot the rules, and tried to join Gan on her Long, Long Road to Tipperary.

CHAPTER
NINE

'Run Rabbit, Run.'
(*Popular War Song*)

Although rationing was an unwelcome restriction on most people's choice of food it didn't, at first, make a great deal of difference to us.

Most of the food we ate was unrationed. Vegetables were plentiful and cheap. Apples were freely given to us by old Mrs Brown who, together with her husband, suffered from ill-fitting teeth and could not chew them, and Mrs Finchcombe as part of a reciprocal deal. We swopped our butter ration for Mrs Finchcombe's margarine and as many apples as we wanted. Mrs Timble bought our cheese ration, Gan assuring her that none of us liked cheese, which was true enough at the time, because we had never tasted it.

We seldom took our meat ration and never bacon, but occasionally bought liver, tripe and cow-heels, none of which was rationed.

The mainstay of our meat diet was still rabbit, but Gan was beginning to suffer qualms. Whether or not to continue accepting rabbits from Tilda's friend George became a vexed question, on which she and Mum did not agree.

It was about this time that Diane and I first became aware of a secret language spoken between Mum and Gan. We soon realised that sections of their conversations which they did not wish us to understand, were spoken in this code. It was, in fact, the relatively simple one of dropping the initial sound of any key word, and adding it to the end. However, it needed a stroke of luck before I cracked it.

Mum and Gan became remarkably fluent in their use of this ploy, able to rattle off at will what seemed utter gibberish to us.

One Saturday afternoon I was dressed ready to go out and trying not to look at the table where Gan had put the pathetic little furry creature that Tilda Hawkins had just brought in. Mum was getting Jill ready while Diane pretended to look for her other glove.

"I don't know whether we should go on taking these rabbits," Gan began.

"Why ever not?" Mum on her knees, fastening Jill's shoes, looked up in surprise.

"Because I don't trust that . . ." Gan broke off and shot me an irritated glance. "What are you hanging about for, Betty? Are you getting ready?"

"I'm ready." Recognising that she was annoyed with me whether I was ready or not, I moved back, further away from her and the rabbit.

Gan said to Mum, every word clearly emphasised, "I ouldn't-w ive-g that ighter-bl the slightest cuse-ex to do eg-Gr down."

Mum stopped to think, before saying quickly, "I'm sure he wouldn't, Mum. He's eg-Gr's best iend-fr."

Gan snorted. "Iend-fr? If you believe that you'll believe anything. I tell you, ilda-T ooked-l a darn sight too eased-pl ith-w herself this orning-m."

Mum got to her feet and retied the strings of Jill's pixie hat, which she had pulled undone.

"I don't see what difference it will make if we don't buy his rabbits," she said.

"Shsh." Gan gave her a frowning look and me another irritable one. I hastily began to help Diane look for her glove, though I knew she had lost it on our last walk past the Wiggle Farm geese.

"The difference is, it's beginning to feel too much like taking advantage of moral-im nings-ear."

"Oh Mum!" I could hear the shock in Mum's voice. "I'm sure she's not . . . they aren't . . . Besides, you can hardly call a sixpenny rabbit moral-im nings-ear."

"That's not the point. I can't watch ilda-T sking-a for ouble-tr and not do anything to op-st her."

Mum said, firmly for her, "It's nothing to do with us." But Gan angrily contradicted her.

"It damn well is. I promised eg-Gr I'd eep-k an eye on ilda-T while he was away. I'm not letting that ighter-bl . . ."

I had made the mistake of turning to stare at her in open fascination, and she furiously swallowed the rest of her words.

"What are you two doing?"

"W . . . we're l . . . l . . . looking for Di . . . Diane's gl . . . glove," I stammered and Diane's lip began to tremble.

"Well it won't be floating about in the air, will it? Go and look upstairs."

It wouldn't be upstairs either, as we knew only too well. But we both made a dive for the door to the stairs, and heard no more of Gan's intriguing nings-ear and ighter-bl's.

Diane managed to hide the loss of her glove and we set off on one of our frequent foraging expeditions. This one was for elderberries, for Gan to make into wine.

She made good wines and jams, in sharp contrast to her ineptitude at more basic cookery. So every autumn we eagerly picked elderberries, blackberries and sloes from the hedges, loganberries from our own garden, and for weeks afterwards the house was full of the sweet smells of fermenting wine and boiling jam.

We children loved her jam, though it was always the subject of an 'either . . . or'. We could either have jam on our bread or margarine, but not both. I remember once when she didn't give us a choice, denying us jam for ages in a fit of pique.

She had given Diane and me our usual thick slice of bread for tea, liberally spread with loganberry jam. To my horror, there was a wasp in mine.

I told Gan and she flatly contradicted me. "Nonsense, it's a big loganberry. Get it down you!" she insisted.

"B . . . but it is." Tears welled up in my eyes and exasperated, Gan flounced over to look at my plate. Nobody else had said a word.

One of Gan's most obstinate traits was an absolute inability ever to admit she was in the wrong. She could insist black was white, or, in this case, a loganberry had black and yellow stripes, refusing to accept the evidence of her own eyes. And that was that. She didn't make me eat it, but she threw away the whole jar of jam in temper, and for a week or so, Diane and I were given margarine on our bread in stony silence, until she eventually relented.

Our walk that afternoon was in the direction of Whitsands. Evidence of war was everywhere. Every now and then we came across a pill-box hidden in the tall hedge, with a soldier standing guard. One of them asked us to produce our identity cards, though he could hardly have thought two women and three children posed any threat.

Up on the military road along the cliffs, Army lorries brought soldiers and their ammunition to and from Tregantle Fort and we could see barrage balloons floating over Rame Head and on Maker Heights. Rame Head was a promontory overlooking Plymouth Breakwater. Public access was now denied on the Head and soldiers, guns and barbed wire were all over it.

We could see no submarines out in the bay, only a solitary warship getting smaller and smaller as it steamed towards Eddystone Lighthouse. We turned back down Donkey Lane and filled three bags with elderberries.

We arrived home to find there was a long, tarpaulin-covered vehicle stuck outside our house, one

of its huge wheels jammed against our white-washed corner rubbing-stone.

Mrs Finchcombe was hovering anxiously on her doorstep. "You'll be careful, won't you," she was entreating the driver, dismayed that he wasn't even looking at her cottage, a foot from his front wheel.

His attention was directed behind him as he bellowed out, "How many more inches, Jack?" Jack, standing opposite our front door, yelled back, "A good three or four, Bert," and it was Gan's turn to feel alarm.

"Just a minute!" she called across to Jack. "Another four inches and you'll be in our living-room," but the soldier was undeterred.

"Don't you worry, Missus, we know what we're doing." He waved a large, horny hand to the driver. "Back a bit, Bert. A bit more. STOP!" He turned to grin at Mum and Gan. "You see! Always trust the British Army, ladies."

Though they had got the wheel free of the corner-stone, we knew from experience that getting round into Dodbrook would be a long-drawn-out manoeuvre. We squeezed round the vehicle to our front door and found Tilda at her front door, chatting to two soldiers.

The genial smile with which Gan had rewarded Jack stayed on her face. But we were always very sensitive to her moods. She was not best pleased.

"A cup of tea, lads?" she suggested and the men eagerly accepted.

"Are you coming too?" the tall, fair-haired one asked Tilda.

"Oh . . . but I don't know if Mrs Cooper . . ." Tilda looked at Gan with a prettily hesitant smile and Gan had no alternative but to invite her in.

Our little room was crowded. Diane and I sat on the bottom stair and between us took off Jill's outdoor clothes. Mum made the tea, because Gan seemed more concerned with Tilda's comfort.

"Come and sit next to me," she smiled and Tilda slowly removed herself from the friendly arm the tall soldier had placed behind her shoulders and did as she was bid.

Gan indicated the other two chairs for the men. "Mrs Hawkins' husband is fighting somewhere in the Middle East," she told them.

The tall one looked sympathetically at Tilda. "That's hard. You must be very lonely."

"Oh yes," Tilda sighed. "I do miss him."

"And I'm sure he misses you," Gan said quickly. "Thinking about you to come back to is what's keeping him going."

"I think it's hardest for the women," said Tilda's champion and he earned a grateful smile from her wide blue eyes.

"Yes, it . . ."

"No, it isn't!" Gan contradicted. "It's hardest for the men away from home. It must mean a lot to them to know that their wives are waiting for them."

Mum brought in a tray of tea, to find all four chairs occupied. The short, stocky soldier, who had not yet said a word, grinned, "There's room on my knee," then caught Gan's icy expression and hastily got to his feet.

"You sit here," he mumbled.

We had become used to entertaining stranded soldiers, as had our neighbours, while the vehicle crews struggled, often for an hour or more, to get a twenty- or thirty-foot unarticulated vehicle round a street corner built to accommodate a horse and cart. But this occasion lacked the goodwill and cheerfulness of all the others. No one took any notice of Diane and me. Even three-year-old Jill, always sure of being picked up and held squealing in the air above some khaki-clad figure, was ignored when she trotted over to stare hopefully up at them. For some reason, Gan was in one of her moods, and that was enough to put a damper on everyone within reach of her.

Tilda stood up. "Thanks for the tea, Mrs Cooper. I must go and pick up Andy from Mrs Dewey's, just up the road."

Her sweet smile included the two soldiers, but lingered on the tall one. "I'm always nervous of being out in the blackout," she confessed.

The soldier shot to his feet. "Come on, I'll walk you there and back," he offered.

Gan's expression of disapproval started a reciprocal qualm in my stomach. Was she going to start one of her devastating rows?

"But what about your lorry? Surely it will be round that corner any time now?"

"It'll take at least another half hour," the soldier cheerfully told her. "We always allow an hour to get through Millbrook."

Off they went, while Mum saw the other one out. She came back to an explosive release of Gan's pent-up feelings.

"That little fool'll be the death of me," she flared out. "Whoever would have thought she was man-mad?"

"Oh, I'm sure she's not." Mum attempted to appease. "She's just lonely, if you ask me."

"Well, I didn't ask you!" Diane and I exchanged alarmed glances. Gan was going to have a row with Mum, and we would be next. We sidled past her as she icily told Mum, "And you were no better than you should be, letting that soldier squeeze you where he shouldn't. I don't know what young women are coming to. Let them set eyes on a khaki uniform and they go mad."

We were out, thankfully scampering up the stone steps to our long, narrow garden to play with the cat, leaving Mum to stick up for herself, though we knew she wouldn't.

CHAPTER
TEN

'Keep the Home Fires Burning.'
(*Popular War Song*)

We were inveterate foragers. As well as the abundant fruit from the hedgerows we also gathered thistledown that autumn of 1940, from along the cliffs. It was to make a pillow for Jill and we were amazed at how many bagfuls it took.

Diane and I shared other children's delight in saving bits of shrapnel and aeroplane, between which we couldn't always tell the difference. We also found used machine-gun bullet cases.

For several weeks we regularly found an egg in the hedge. Diane had stumbled on it by chance, on the day she found her lost glove in the lane past Wiggle Farm. Though eggs were not yet rationed it was a real find, despite it giving Gan an excuse for outfacing the geese more often than we liked. She said if we didn't go regularly, the hen would start laying the egg in a different place. It did too, eventually.

But our most frequent sorties were in search of wood. Coal was in short supply but in any case, we couldn't afford to buy enough to keep our fires going.

We couldn't afford the services of a chimney sweep either, when the chimney began belching smoke into our living-room. "It's no good, I'll have to fire it," Gan announced.

She did it one afternoon, while Diane and I were at school. Coming home in the early dusk, we could see sparks shooting out of our chimney, in the midst of a column of black smoke.

Mum and Gan were in a panic when we hurried into the house, with the predictable result; Gan was blaming Mum for what had happened.

"It's never gone like that before. You should never have let the whole of that sheet of newspaper fly up the chimney. I told you, Ida, a bit at a time." Gan was red-faced and flustered, sweeping up lumps of soot which had fallen on the hearth-rug.

"Here, take Jill upstairs to play while we clean up, there's a good girl." Mum distractedly thrust Jill's hand into Diane's and began picking up bits of charred newspaper.

In the middle of all this, there was a loud knock on the door and Gan shot over to the window, the brush and shovel still in her hand.

"Drat the man, it's Mr Brown," she hissed. "Don't say a word, Ida. Leave it to me."

She shoved the brush and shovel at me and told me to take them to the wash-house. When I returned, Mr Brown was surveying the evidence of soot and burnt paper, a scandalised expression on his face.

"Mrs Cooper, you've never gone and set your chimney on fire, with a war on? I couldn't believe my eyes when I looked out of Dicken's window." Dicken's was the bakery in West Street where he worked.

Through having hurried straight to our house from Dicken's, Mr Brown lacked the official trappings of tin-hat and arm-band. But his air of stern authority was enough to stem Gan's ready flow of excuses. That, and the fact that he wasn't listening.

"It was a piece of paper, accidentally flew up the chimney, Mr Brown. We didn't . . ."

"Whatever were you thinking of? There's enough sparks coming out of your chimney to bring a whole squadron of Nazi bombers to Millbrook." Mr Brown shook his grey-haired head in disbelief.

"As I'm trying to tell you, Mr Brown . . ."

Mr Brown's eyes had come to rest on Mum, pieces of scorched paper in her hands.

"You didn't ought to let your mother do such dangerous things," he reproved her.

Mum, quite speechless, cast an apprehensive glance at Gan's scarlet face. Gan looked as though she was about to ignite herself. Her voice was rising. "I was just going to douse the fire when you knocked on the door. Go and get a bucket of water, Ida."

Mr Brown was a kindly man. Before Mum could move to obey he patted her shoulder. "No need to look so upset, m'dear. Just you go and get something to dampen it down with, before the blackout, and we'll say no more about it."

When Mr Brown looked at Gan, her lips had closed, silenced, in a tight, thin line. Her high colour had intensified the dark, steel grey of her eyes, while her thick grey hair, cut short and fashionably waved, emphasised the strong, assertive lines of her face. She looked anything but the archetypal old lady who merited indulgence.

Short-sighted Mr Brown, six feet away in his stance by the door, misread her. He adopted a playful tone which he might have used to a child. And he spoke loudly, as though to a deaf one.

"Now don't you go doing that again, Mrs Cooper, or you're going to land yourself in trouble. I'll be off now and leave your daughter to sort you out."

Even I, young as I was, knew he had said the wrong thing. Gan could not bear to be patronised. As Mr Brown turned away towards the door, she exploded.

"Damn and blast it, if you'd just listen to what I was trying to tell you!"

I'd never seen Mum move so fast. Gan had got no further than the 'blast' before she had the warden through the door, her gentle but firm hand on his arm.

"We're really sorry, Mr Brown," she smiled at him. "We'll get the fire dampened down straight away, and I can promise you, it won't happen again."

Her smile had disappeared when she came back in. She gave Gan a nervous glance and was greeted with an icy silence which lasted less than ten seconds before Gan turned on her.

"What the Devil do you mean, you promise it won't happen again? And why should that silly old fool take it for granted that it was my fault, that's what I want to know!"

Mum would never have had the nerve to say, "Well it was, wasn't it?"

Without a word she went to the wash-house, coming back with a bucket of water. She poured it on the fire, sending clouds of steam and a strong smell of sulphur into the room.

Her reticence left Gan with no one to berate except me. "What did you do with the soot?" she barked at me.

"I . . . I left it in the sh . . . shovel."

She whirled off to the wash-house. I was still dithering over whether to slip past her into the garden, to play with Winkle, or to take the coward's course and nip upstairs to join Diane and Jill, when she returned.

"I've put it in a tin on the sink," she announced in her 'And I'll brook no argument' voice. "It's for you and Diane to clean your teeth with."

I must have looked as incredulous as I felt.

"Don't you look at me like that, my girl," she rapped. "It's well known that cleaning your teeth with soot makes them white."

We took her word for it. It would have been unthinkable to have done otherwise. But thankfully, that was one of her fads which did not last long.

With never enough fuel, which was due as much to our poverty as to war-time shortages, bathing was a once a week ritual. It involved a lot of work too. We had a tin bath which hung on the wall in the wash-house. Every Saturday, after tea, Gan set it on the hearth-rug in front of the fire and she and Mum trotted to and from the copper in the wash-house with buckets of water.

Jill was always bathed first, then Diane, then me, all in the same water. I can't remember feeling badly done-to, always being last, until one day, as I watched Jill enjoying her ablutions, I was convinced she wee'd in the water.

Needless to say, Gan would not believe me. She was furious. I suppose she couldn't bear the thought of emptying all those buckets of water and starting again.

"Of course she hasn't. Don't talk such nonsense," she sharply reprimanded me without even looking at Jill's sudden stillness and the distinctly guilty expression in her wide blue eyes. Even Mum was cross with me when Jill's happy gurgles changed to a trembling lip and great tears welled out of her eyes.

"And don't you dare say anything to upset Diane," Gan hissed as we heard Diane returning from the outside lavatory. Even at eight years old Diane would have rebelled at being bathed in possibly polluted water. I was more chicken-hearted, with some of my mother's acceptance of anything for a quiet life.

We were always short of soap, long before it was rationed. Every little bit was saved and remoulded and the last remnants were put into an empty tin with holes pierced in its lid, to use for washing the dishes.

Being hard-up did not mean neighbours would not borrow from us. Gan had a fierce pride in no one knowing just how poverty-stricken we were and she never refused to lend.

Mrs Timble once got our last piece of soap, just before bath night. We ended up with a swish of the washing-up tin, a dash of vinegar and a sprinkling of salt in the water, and firm assurance from Gan that vinegar killed grease and salt killed germs.

Mrs Timble had a tale to tell of Mrs Murdoch.

"I'm sure she's pinching some of my washing, Mrs Cooper. Twice there's been something missing and I've seen her watching from her bedroom window when I've been hanging it out."

"What was missing?" Gan asked, as she wrapped our soap in a piece of newspaper.

Mrs Timble tittered. "Two pairs of bloomers and my best winceyette nightdress."

Tact was never one of Gan's strongest traits. "Well, Good Lord, why would she want your bloomers? She's only half your size, she'd never get them to stay up." She added a final coup de grâce. "Unless she wanted them for dusters, of course."

Even a sycophantic Mrs Timble could not be expected to take that. "I must be getting back to see what the kids are up to," she said stiffly, and made her way to the door, outraged dignity in every line of her short, plump figure. But she relented sufficiently to come back for the soap.

CHAPTER
ELEVEN

'Camouflage your torches.'
(*Government Instruction*)

In that same autumn, Mum started work in Devonport Dockyard, where women were being recruited to take over as the men were called-up. She was taken on as a driller, to work on huge sheets of steel for construction and repair of warships.

Her first few weeks were particularly hard. They coincided with a spate of 'nuisance' raids, not bad enough to bring us out of bed to the wash-house but sufficiently noisy to waken us. One night I emerged from beneath the rag-rug to see Mum and Gan standing at our bedroom window. For a moment I was petrified at the sight of the two sharply silhouetted figures but Gan called softly to me, "Come and see, but don't wake Diane."

They were watching an aircraft trapped in the intersection of two searchlights, anti-aircraft guns from the cliff gun-sites trying to bring it down. As we watched, it escaped its snare, to disappear into the darkness.

That was one of several nights of broken sleep for Mum in those first exacting weeks of her new job, for which she had to get up at 5.30 in the morning.

Mr Brown had offered to knock her up since he had to be at his work in the bakery very early. Mum was very grateful, but the arrangement was not without its teething problems.

In the first few days when Mr Brown woke Mum, he woke us all. His summons didn't stop at a reasonable rattle of the letter box. As Mum lay in bed trying to will herself out of it, Mr Brown gave up on the letter box and started hammering on the door. He didn't stop knocking until Mum had staggered downstairs and peered round the door to tell him she was up.

He was unbearably hearty. "Up you get, rise and shine," he exhorted.

"Yes, I was up. Thank you Mr Brown. If you could just give two or three knocks on the letter box, I'll always hear you."

In the dark, black-outed morning, the old man could not see her face.

"It's a pleasure, m'dear. You've no call to thank me." He trotted back to his own house and breakfast.

The same thing happened for the rest of that week, with slight variations. Mr Brown was very punctual, very noisy, and he would not give up until Mum showed herself at the front door.

She tried calling to him from the bedroom window, at Gan's suggestion. "For heaven's sake, Ida, shout down and tell him you're up," she begged.

Mum obediently put her head out of the window.

"Thank you, Mr Brown . . ." Bang, bang. "Mr Brown, I'm up, thank you . . ." Bang, bang, bang. Mr Brown did not look up and Gan lost her temper.

"I didn't say wake the whole street up! Get downstairs and shut him up."

We could all hear the disconnected dialogue at the door.

"There you are! Thought you were never going to wake up this morning, young woman."

"I was calling to you from the window, Mr Brown . . ."

"You don't like getting out of that nice warm bed now, do you?"

"I was out of it, Mr Brown, you just . . ."

"Never you mind, I'll make sure you don't oversleep."

"Mr Brown . . ."

"Same time tomorrow, m'dear."

We heard the door close and Mum's defeated footsteps as she slowly climbed the stairs.

The problem was solved when she applied for, and got, a permit for an alarm clock.

Mr Brown was a little hurt. "I don't know what you want with one of them," he reproached her. "I'm sure I can make as much noise as an alarm clock."

Though Millbrook was only a few miles from Devonport, on the opposite side of the Tamar, Mum's journey there was difficult. We lived at the head of a tidal creek and the tide determined where the *Western Belle* picked up her passengers. There were four picking-up points. At high tide the boat came right up to the village, but when the tide was out she could only reach the jetty at Southdown about two miles away.

Often strong south-westerlies lashed across the exposed estuary, which Mum always had to cross in the dark, both going and coming home.

The first effect her job had on us children was that we only saw her at weekends. Gan had us in bed by six o'clock each evening. I suppose she thought Mum would be too tired to be bothered with us, and she was probably right.

The work was physically and mentally draining. Mum had to stand all day at a huge drilling machine, which bored holes into the sheet of metal on which she was standing.

The mental stress came at night, when she began to have nightmares, imagining ships sinking with water pouring in through holes she had bored in the wrong place. Thankfully, in time she was able to stop worrying.

Gan must have felt the stress of coping with three children on her own, and we suffered for it. She began to throw things and though she always missed us, we couldn't be sure she would.

Feeling she had been snubbed by Mr Martin, the butcher, Gan refused to go to his shop again and sent me.

She was never satisfied with what I brought, and I was quick to learn from experience. She only had to throw the meat at me once, before I developed the speed of Gonzales. By the time she had torn off the paper and had started exclaiming about it being all fat, all gristle, or all bone, I was past her, out through the wash-house and into the lavatory, often with the thud of the meat hitting the door I had just passed through to convince me it had been a close thing.

Gan threw other things, mostly at the wall. She once threw the primus, after spending ten minutes in an unsuccessful attempt to get it working. Diane and I saw the signs, as her pumping got more violent and her face a deeper crimson, and we were both through the door before it hit the wall, cravenly leaving poor little Jill trapped in her high-chair at the table.

The thing which Gan threw most often was her metal money box, a model of the Bank of England. She had lost its key and was forever trying to get money out of it on a knife blade. This occupation made her swear, though she never said anything worse than 'Damn and Blast' and, when she wanted to be really vehement, 'Bum!' Then the money box would go flying against the wall. It must have been well constructed, for it never broke.

Perhaps throwing things relieved her feelings, but it made Diane, Jill and me very nervous children. Jill, little more than a baby though she was, watched Gan with big, wary blue eyes. Diane and I began to close up like clams, whenever we were with her.

This had both a good and a bad effect on me. Through no longer rushing to get out my words before Gan squashed me, I lost my stutter. But I began to talk more at school, to compensate for the silence at home, and I became more and more drawn into telling lies.

They must have been more obvious than I realised because my teacher, Miss Croft, started to show a closer than usual concern in my moral development. She was kind and very religious. Through her strictures, and the heady sensation of seeming important to someone, I began to adopt her religious beliefs. Ironically, this got me into as much trouble with Gan as any of my tallest stories.

The one I told at school about Uncle Stanley was not particularly spectacular. Uncle Stanley was not a real uncle. He had been a steward on the *Mauretania* who had married Mum's best friend, Thelma, and they had gone to live in America several years before the war began.

Miss Croft asked if any of us had a foreign relative we could tell about to the rest of the class. I obliged with Uncle Stanley, though I had to make up most of it as I had been only three or four when I had last seen him. I also promoted him from steward to Captain.

The following day, when I got home from school, Gan confronted me as soon as I walked through the door.

"What's this rigmarole you've been telling at school about your Uncle Stanley?" she demanded.

I was dumfounded. How had she found out about it?

She had heard through Mrs Timble, whose daughter Eva was in my class.

"Why the Devil did you say he was a Captain when you know he wasn't?"

"I . . . I th . . . thought . . ." Surely I wasn't going to start stammering again. I shut up, to stare dumbly into Gan's icy grey eyes.

"You thought? You thought no such thing! It's just another of your lies, isn't it? Just you trying to be big. Isn't it?"

It was true, what she said. A Captain had sounded much more exciting than a steward and all the class had been impressed.

Though Miss Croft's reaction to my interesting American relative had been disappointing. When she called me to her desk with my work, instead of enquiring more about Uncle Stanley, as I expected, she had asked me quietly and kindly if I was remembering to ask for God's guidance in my prayers. "You know He always wants us to speak the truth?"

She could not possibly know anything about Uncle Stanley but my sharpening conscience pricked me. Miss Croft told me gently, "Be sure God will always forgive you as long as you are sorry, Betty."

I looked at Gan's accusing face and blurted out, "God will forgive me."

If I had invoked the Devil himself, it could not have had a more sensational effect. Gan was so astounded, it was several seconds before she found her voice. When she did she frightened the life out of all three of us. "You cheeky little Madam!" she shouted at me.

Diane recovered first and shot out to the lavatory, while Jill's tuneless crooning to her shabby little Teddy Bear stopped in mid-note, as she stared over its head at Gan with startled eyes.

I thought Gan was going to slap me and cowered into the coats hanging on the door-peg behind me.

I must have looked abject enough to quell even her temper. Impatiently she exclaimed, "For heaven's sake, anyone would think I was going to murder you." It was exactly what I did think, and I breathed a frantic prayer for Divine help, though with enough sense not to let her hear it.

Exasperated, she snapped, "Oh, get away from that door. And if you want to say your prayers, you'd better ask the Lord to keep my hands from around your neck."

I couldn't believe it. As I thankfully scurried away from my tight corner, I earnestly assured her, "I just did."

I knew immediately that I had said the wrong thing again. But I was no longer cornered amongst the coats and before Gan could make another move I was outside, hammering on the lavatory door, bawling to Diane with perfect truth, that I was desperate.

Mr Brown called one Saturday morning, when Mum had been working for two or three weeks. In addition to an alarm clock permit, Mum had been issued with one entitling her to a torch, and he came to make sure that she knew the regulations concerning its use.

Gan, rarely pleased to see unexpected callers, was even more annoyed because she was halfway through skinning a rabbit. She impatiently gathered up the furry little body which the rest of us had been trying to avoid looking at, wrapped it in newspaper, and took it out to the wash-house, leaving Mum to deal with Mr Brown.

He had brought a piece of tissue paper and proceeded to insert it under the glass of her torch.

"There, that'll stop them Nazis from aiming one of their bombs on you, m'dear," he told her. "They'd have to be flying at twenty feet to see that."

Mum looked at the almost non-existent glimmer of light from her torch. "Are you sure it needs two thicknesses of tissue paper, Mr Brown?" she asked. "I don't think I'll be able to see as much as *ten* feet in front of me with this."

Mr Brown was admiring his own handiwork. "Some folk put a dark patch under the glass, with a hole in it. But tissue paper gives a broader light."

"Mr Brown!" Mum put her hand on his arm, drawing his gaze. She spoke clearly. "Wouldn't one thickness of tissue be enough? It seems a waste of the battery to get such little light from it."

"Now you leave it how I've done it, m'dear," Mr Brown said earnestly. "Isn't it better not to be able to see where you're going, than to have bombs dropped on you?"

"Well yes, but . . ."

"It's regulations, young woman." The warden's voice became more authoritative. "And another thing, you must never shine it upwards, only onto the ground in front of you."

The old man put the torch onto the table, where a solemn-faced Jill was standing watching him. He chucked her under the chin. "Did you see the story in the *Herald* of that soldier who was caught flashing his torch in the woods?"

"No, we don't get . . ."

"You couldn't have missed it. It was on the front page. Well, well, you're a serious little maid, aren't you?" Jill stared up at him, clutching tighter to her Teddy. Mr Brown gave up and looked at Mum.

"He said he was trying to find the path but if you ask me, he was up to no good. There was a young woman with him." He coughed. "Anyway, he was sentenced to a month in prison."

Mum was startled. "Good gracious! That seems a lot for just flashing a torch."

"He should have got six months," Mr Brown said severely. "There were enemy aircraft flying over at the time. It would have served him right if they had dropped one on him. Anyway," disapproval slowed his words, "I've just heard the fellow appealed against the sentence and the Magistrates changed it to a five pound fine. So don't you go worrying about a tuppenny battery, m'dear. It's better than five pounds any day."

Mum began to explain, "It wasn't really the cost of the battery I was bothered about, just that . . ." But she had lost the old man's attention.

He was looking at the sideboard. "That alarm clock's ten minutes slow," he said, and there was unmistakable satisfaction in his voice. "No wonder you nearly missed the boat yesterday morning. Now you never did that when I was calling you up, did you!"

He did not wait for an answer, which was just as well, because Mum was lost for words. Gan was not though, when she flounced in as soon as the door had closed behind him.

"That man wouldn't talk so much if you didn't encourage him, Ida," she grumbled.

Mum protested, "I don't encourage him."

"Oh?" Gan's tone was one of triumph. "Then how come I never have any trouble getting shot of him?"

Of course, Mum had no answer for that one either!

CHAPTER
TWELVE

'Bang, Bang, Bang, Bang, goes the Farmer's Gun.'
(*From Run Rabbit, Run*)

A tense situation had developed between Gan and
Tilda Hawkins. Gan felt a fierce loyalty to Greg,
fighting in the Middle East, and would have zealously
guarded his wife's reputation for him, had she been
given the chance. But she wasn't.

"That girl might look as though butter wouldn't
melt in her mouth, but she's a flighty piece under it
all," she snorted. She had been next door to pay for
the last rabbit. "Would you credit it. When I asked her
if she'd rather you dropped the money in at his house,
next time you went to Southdown, she had the nerve
to tell me she was sure to see him before you did! And
that without blinking an eyelid, the brazen little
hussy!"

She caught my interested gaze and said sharply, "Go
and see if the cat's come back."

"It hasn't. I've just been out to look."

"Well go and look again." As I went through the
wash-house, leaving an absorbed Diane playing with
some dominoes on the floor with Jill, I heard Gan say,
"He as-w in gain-a ast-l ight-n."

I walked slowly. Mum said, "He would have been out on fire-watching last night, even though the raid over Plymouth was a short one." She paused. "He probably ame-c to ee-s if e-sh as-w right-al."

If e-sh as-w right-al? In a flash I recognised "right-al" as 'all right'. As I continued out to the backyard I heard Gan's sarcastic voice. "To ee-s if e-sh as-w right-al? More like *or-f* a it-b of right-al, if you ask me."

I walked slowly up the steps and along the garden path. There was no sign of Winkle. If "right-al" meant "all right", then "it-b" was . . . "bit"! I thought of the words I could remember, and changed the position of the syllables. Elated, I realised that I had cracked the code, though Gan's remarks still made little sense to me. "A bit of all right"? All I understood was that she had been talking about Tilda Hawkins, and someone who had come to visit her in the night.

It was Sunday, and the rabbit had been stewing on the range all morning. Potatoes and carrots boiled alongside it.

Gan never felt the need to introduce a little variety into her cooking, despite a number of helpful suggestions from Lord Woolton. He was the Minister of Food, in whose name Food Facts were issued regularly in the daily papers. Gan had torn a few of them out of the newspaper salvage I collected for Miss Croft, but only so that she could ridicule them.

"Look at this!" she exclaimed once. "Kedgeree of kidneys! And where does he think I'm going to get kidneys, with a butcher like we've got?"

A recipe for rabbit pudding had incensed her even more. "You can tell a man's concocted this," she had scorned. "Does he think I've nothing better to do than make a pudding to put the rabbit in, when it tastes just as good straight out of the pot?" She had never had a good word to say for Lord Woolton, since he announced tea rationing on the wireless, without warning, when she had been on her last packet.

We had our Sunday meal, ravenously eating up all the hard little cubes of carrot and every lump of watery potato, from plates swimming with so much thin rabbit gravy we had to eat it with spoons. But it satisfied our hunger and we cheerfully set off on a wood-collecting expedition, despite the squally rain which had been falling all morning.

Thankfully, even Gan could not face wind, rain and the geese all at once, so we avoided Wiggle Farm. We walked along the cliffs as far as Rame Head, where a sentry on guard at the camp there prevented us from going any further, and returned back down Donkey Lane to collect the wood.

Diane and I were in bed by six o'clock, as usual. We could never get to sleep straight away. For a while we lay listening to the sounds of the wireless downstairs, cheerful music, or the quiet tones of a man reading the news. We had once heard the King's voice, telling us to be courageous and such was the patriotism instilled into us, Diane and I solemnly stood up on our bed, as the National Anthem was played.

98

I had learned to read very early, constantly encouraged by Miss Croft, to Gan's annoyance. "What does she want to turn you into a bookworm for?" she grumbled. "You live in a world of your own as it is."

Reading did indeed transport me to another, more exciting world.

During the light nights I had started reading to Diane when we were in bed but the early darkness of winter prevented that. So I began to make up stories, my voice droning on beneath the bedclothes until one or the other of us fell asleep. I often continued the story the following night, from where I had left off.

There was a raid that Sunday night. It was not a heavy one but the enemy must have been overhead because we woke to the short, sharp blasts of PC

Polworthy's whistle. Gan came to tell us to stay where we were. She was still dressed, so she and Mum had not yet come to bed. While she was still in the room we heard a plane roar low over the village and a minute later, heard it crash.

Diane and I shot out of bed and rushed to join Gan at the window. We heard Mum's quick feet on the stairs as she ran to fetch Jill.

In a pitch black sky, above the sloping fields behind our house, we saw a faint glow, which spread and became brighter as we watched it. And then silence.

Gan said quietly, "That's some poor soul gone to his Maker." But she was wrong, as we found out the next day.

Mum had long gone to work by the time Diane and I got up. We were eating our porridge when Tilda came round from next door.

It had become unusual for Tilda to seek out Gan, apart from when she was delivering a rabbit. She was not a borrower either, though the first thing she said when Gan answered the door was, "Oh, Mrs Cooper, can you lend me a spoon of tea, until I collect my rations?"

Gan looked surprised, but immediately invited her in. "Of course I will, but come and have one with me first," she invited.

Like a child bursting with news, Tilda began her tale even before she had reached the chair next to Diane that Gan was indicating.

"Well, what about last night then, Mrs Cooper! But you won't know the half of it!"

"Do you mean the plane that crashed?" Gan brought another cup and saucer and put milk and sugar into it. "Were you frightened on your own with little Andy? Why don't you come to us when there's a raid, Tilda. We'd always find room for you."

Tilda accepted a cup of the strong, sweet tea. "Don't you worry about us, Mrs Cooper. Andy sleeps through everything, and as for me . . ." She bravely repeated her proud little boast, "Hitler's not going to get me out of my own home, whatever he does!"

She sipped some of Gan's bitter brew and hastily put down her cup. "Anyway Mrs Cooper, guess what! I . . . I happened to see George Dorman last night, on his way back from the police station. You'll never believe this . . . he helped to capture two of the German airmen who had parachuted from that plane last night."

Gan's silence drew my glance to her. Her expression was one of strong disapproval. I stared, baffled until I vaguely remembered a previous conversation with Mum, when Gan had shown a dislike of George Dorman. She was showing it again, though why, when George Dorman was obviously a hero, I could not imagine.

Tilda was too thrilled with her story to be put off by Gan's lack of encouragement. Her cheeks were flushed, emphasising the deep blue of her eyes. I thought she was beautiful.

"It was Joe Benson caught the first one," she said. "He lives next door to George at Southdown. He was in bed asleep, when he was woken up by shots, and there was this German outside, firing his gun. It turned

101

out later he was just trying to attract somebody's attention, but Joe wasn't to know that, was he? Anyway, Joe dashed outside with his rabbit gun, though Mrs Benson tried to stop him, and arrested the German."

Diane and I were listening, enthralled, our cooling porridge setting in a solid bank, like a mud creek invaded by little rivulets of milk. We would never have dared to ask questions and it was obvious that Gan was disinclined. All she said, in a stiff voice was, "Well, I'm glad they weren't burned to death. I wouldn't wish that on any man, German or not."

What had happened to the other one? Had anyone got shot and what part had George Dorman played? Where were the German prisoners now? Excited questions quivered on the tip of my tongue and to my relief Tilda poured out the answers without being asked.

"Well, George heard the commotion from next door and he and his Dad came to give Joe a hand. They'd all got their rabbit guns and the three of them marched the German to the police station and handed him over to PC Polworthy. And what do you think? There was another one already there, who'd been picked up by soldiers at the Rame Head camp. Anyway," Tilda had almost stopped drawing breath, "the one in the police station spoke English and he said there'd been four of them and they'd all baled out. He was the pilot and said they'd lost their way and thought they were over Brest, in France, until he was picked up by the Tommies! Well, like George said, he must have had a rotten navigator."

Gan couldn't resist a scornful comment. "But how could they have thought they were in France, with our gunners shooting at them?"

"But they weren't. The plane got caught in a balloon cable," Tilda eagerly explained. She had got her breath back.

"Anyway, PC Polworthy organised men in pairs to go looking for the other two Germans, so George went off to Hoskins' farm, up at the back of Southdown and called up old Frank Hoskins. They went out with their guns and when they got to the turnip field, they heard someone shouting for help and there was this German with a twisted ankle. So they carried him to the farm and Mrs Hoskins gave him a cup of tea and they took his boots off. George says that's so he couldn't escape."

Gan said drily, "I wouldn't have thought he'd get far with a twisted ankle."

Tilda seemed momentarily deflated. "No, I suppose not, but George says you can't be too careful. Anyway . . ." she was off again, "The police arrived to take him to the police station and George was thanked particularly by PC Polworthy for all his help."

Gan said stiffly, "You seem to have got the whole tale, right down to the last details, Tilda."

"Yes," Tilda blandly agreed. "Wasn't it lucky that I happened to be looking out of the window just as George was passing? I must see if I can catch him again, to find out if they've caught the fourth man."

Gan had just noticed Diane's and my absorbed faces. She said sharply, "Finish that porridge and get your coats, you two. You'll be late for school." We hastily scraped off the last encrusted porridge adhering to the sides of our bowls, and scurried around collecting hats and coats, gas-masks and a large bundle of newspapers I had collected for Miss Croft.

Tilda had gone by the time we were ready for school. Gan was too incensed to respond to our dutiful goodbyes. "I *knew* she hadn't really come round for a spoonful of tea," was all we got.

As soon as we stepped outside, we could see there was some sort of a row going on outside the police station, only a short way up the road from our house. Three or four of the village women were passing on some forceful opinions to PC Polworthy, who was standing on the station step. The only one we could hear was Mrs Dobson, who had a louder voice than anyone else.

The policeman's gaze was fixed on her. "Now then, Mrs Dobson," he asked sternly. "What's all this about?"

"Let's have a look at those German prisoners you've got." She cast a bold glance about her and got a babble of support from her cronies. "We want to see what men look like, that drop bombs on innocent children."

"They don't look any different to our pilots, who are dropping bombs on German children," PC Polworthy told her firmly. "Now, I have to ask you to disperse, ladies. You are causing a nuisance."

Mrs Dobson was not finished. "They started it."

"And we're going to finish it. Now will you please go home."

"That's all very well." Mrs Dobson's eyes rolled towards Mrs Pendennis, who had started to move away. "We still think . . ."

"That reminds me, Mrs Dobson." The policeman interrupted her. "Tell your husband I'll be round to see him later this morning. He'll know what it's about."

Mrs Dobson instantly bridled, before casting another fierce glance at her dwindling supporters. This time, her belligerence was directed against them, and in particular at old Mrs Brown, who had just dragged herself out of her house to see what was going on.

"And you needn't give me that look," the rag-and-bone man's wife shouted towards the flustered old lady. "My Alf has done nothing to be ashamed of, and I'll give him what for if he has."

Then, quite suddenly, they'd all gone except Mrs Dobson. Mrs Brown turned round and shuffled back to her house and PC Polworthy went back inside his police station after a final warning to Mrs Dobson. As she began to make her way towards us, Diane and I had the same instant thought, that we'd better get going before Gan came out to see what was going on.

We were late for school, but the excitement had been worth it. Miss Croft wanted to know why I was late.

"There was this huge crowd of women outside the police station, all shouting at PC Polworthy to throw out the German prisoners," I told her. I'm sure she did not believe me.

CHAPTER
THIRTEEN

'Careless Talk Costs Lives.'
(*Government Poster*)

It was several days before I found out what had happened to the fourth German airman. All that week I kept getting tantalising snippets of information, eagerly passing these on to Gan when I got home from school.

I should have known better, but the longing to repeat an exciting tale was irresistible. Like the proverbial boy who cried wolf too often, I got my just desserts. Gan was always ready to hear any news I brought from school, but was just as quick to disbelieve it.

"He came down in the sea at Cawsand." I had got this from Mary Penhallow. "He nearly got drowned and was saved by two Cawsand fishermen."

The following day I reported another instalment, this time from Eva Timble.

"Eva Timble says the fishermen's boat nearly sank as they were dragging the German in, because he was tangled up in his parachute. Hundreds of people were standing on the beach and cheering as they just got the boat back before it sank. Eva says one of the fishermen is married to her second cousin's best friend."

Gan said shortly, "If I were you, I'd be careful what tales I told about Eva Timble. I haven't forgotten the last tale *she* brought home to her mother, about *you*."

I had not forgotten either and that was the end of my news bulletins. When Effie Dewey told me her Dad had seen a huge hole in the men's boat, after they had landed the half-drowned airman, I only told Diane.

Then one day, Gan met us at the door when we arrived home for lunch. "Get that down you quickly," she ordered, indicating the bowls of Oxo and fingers of bread laid out on the newspaper-covered table. "I've heard Elton's have got some dried fruit in. I'll go down with you on your way back to school and you can look after Jill while I'm in the queue." She was getting Jill's coat on before we'd dunked the first bread finger.

In one particular respect, Gan was very different to the other village women. She never left Diane and me at home to look after Jill, or allowed us to take her out unaccompanied. She was loudly critical of women who pushed baby-minding duties on to their older children, though I think there was also an element in her attitude of denying us any loosening of her apron-strings. She kept a tight control over where we could or could not go and making friends with other children was firmly discouraged. It meant that we grew up into a very insular family, always turned in on ourselves.

On her way out of the shop, Gan came face to face with Mrs Pendennis. The two women had not spoken to one another since their fall-out in the butcher's queue over Mrs Pendennis's friend, Hilda. On this occasion, Gan made the first move to reconciliation.

She said gruffly, "If you get in the queue quickly, Mrs Pendennis, they've got some rice as well as dried fruit."

The other woman was quick to seize the olive branch. "Well, isn't that just my luck, Mrs Cooper," she smiled. "I've used all me this month's points."

Gan tutted in sympathy. "I was talking to Mrs Timble last week. I hear you've been having trouble with Mrs Murdoch. That woman's a menace."

With a rapport clearly re-established, the two women moved up West Street together. Gan had apparently forgotten that Diane and I were still there with Jill in her push-chair, waiting to go back to school. We trotted behind her, waiting to be remembered, not daring to interrupt.

"Fancy accusing you of spitting. *She's* the one who spits!"

"I know! That's what I found so hard to take. Said I'd done it on her washing, would you believe, and there's poor old PC Polworthy dragged round again. He must be fed up trying to sort that woman out."

Gan agreed. "I should think he's had more than enough to do, guarding German prisoners, without Mrs Murdoch going off her head again. I expect you heard all about that?"

But Mrs Pendennis had not heard of the Southdown men's exploits. So Gan passed on Tilda's tale with relish, but gave Joe Benson a more heroic part and George Dorman just a mention.

"I still don't know what happened to the fourth man," she admitted. "I've heard so many garbled accounts, it's difficult to know what to believe."

Her words must have brought me to mind. She turned to look at us. "It's time you were off to school. Let me have the push-chair," she ordered.

But before she could grasp its handle, Mrs Pendennis had eagerly begun, "Well, I can tell you about that, Mrs Cooper, because my Bill got the whole story from Tom Trellis, in the Mucky Duck at Cawsand. He was one of the two fishermen who brought the German in, you know."

It wasn't only Gan who was instantly enthralled. I was too. I patiently held on to the push-chair handle while Diane went to press her nose on Dicken's cake shop window and Gan and her friend became once more completely absorbed in one another.

The accounts which I had brought home from school had been remarkably accurate. The noise of the crashing aircraft had brought people in Cawsand, even nearer to Rame Head than we were, rushing down to

110

the beach. There, they could hear cries for help, from out at sea. So Tom Trellis and Herbert Matthews took their boat out to rescue the airman.

"And then," said Mrs Pendennis dramatically, "A hundred yards out from the shoreline they found their boat was leaking. They'd forgotten to put the spike back in ... you know, all boats having to be immobilised in case we're invaded. So Herbert stuck his thumb in the hole, while Tom rowed on."

She cackled, her shaking chins expressing her mirth. "Just like the little Dutch boy!"

"Why ever didn't they turn back?" Gan exclaimed. "They could have been drowned."

"Well, it was a good job they didn't, because the German was already half drowned when they reached him. He was being pulled under by his parachute and the men had a devil of a job getting him into the boat. They started back and it began to fill up with water again. So Herbert looked after the airman, while poor old Tom had to row with one foot over the hole. He told Bill, that's the last time he'll take his spike out, invasion or no invasion."

By the time each Friday night arrived, both Mum and Gan must have been worn out. Thrown into a man's heavy work with no previous idea of what it would be like and with the long hours of travelling to and from the Dockyard, Mum was still finding the first-hand knowledge of crippled ships and men emotionally exhausting.

"Do you know what I find is the worst, Mum," she confessed. "It's seeing all those ships crawl in, badly damaged and knowing there are terribly wounded men on board, and then having to watch them sail out again after we've repaired them. The sight of those sailors standing motionless along the deck as they leave the Yard, makes me want to weep."

"I know." Gan spoke gruffly, as she always did when she was moved. "I saw Mrs Finchcombe on Wednesday. She'd had a letter from Billy and was bursting to tell someone. She was telling me she often goes over to Torpoint to visit her daughter, and she watches the ships sail out and says a prayer for them. She says she hopes someone prays for Billy, when he sails out of Portsmouth on the *Hood*."

Mum told us of seeing half a ship brought in by Lord Louis Mountbatten. Its bow and stern had been blown off and Mum said all the women had wept as the ship, which they knew was HMS *Javelin*, although ships' names were not shown during the war, limped slowly into the dock.

Gan, in her fifties, when most women had finished with child-rearing, had ended up with three grandchildren under nine years of age to look after. To make matters worse, all three of us had gone down with measles, mumps, whooping cough and chicken pox during 1939/1940, with all the extra work which that entailed.

We were lucky to escape diphtheria. After a number of cases breaking out amongst younger children, all the older ones were immunised at school, and I think it was at that time we were issued with cod-liver oil and malt, which I liked but Diane hated.

So what with illness, exacerbated by poverty, wartime hardships and her impatient temperament, it was a wonder Gan did not actually wring our necks, instead of frequently threatening to.

Air-raids were becoming more frequent, though they were not always very long. We had started buying a newspaper when Mum got her job. Newspaper reports were often censored but when we saw a report of a West Country town having been raided two hundred and two times, we all knew it referred to Plymouth. Sometimes there would be as many as four raids in twenty-four hours and more than once the 'All-clear' hastily changed into the 'Alert', as enemy planes either returned or another lot arrived.

Saltash and Torpoint, both small towns situated across narrower stretches of the River Tamar from Plymouth and Devonport Dockyard, were suffering more direct hits than we were. News of Torpoint came from Mrs Finchcombe, whose daughter's cottage was by the water's edge, within sight of a group of huge oil tanks.

Mrs Finchcombe had been particularly incensed in her telling of the repeated bombing of the Naval Camp, on the outskirts of the town. "How do the Germans know it's there?" she demanded indignantly. "It's too well camouflaged to see from the air. I think it's spies!!"

Fear of careless talk helping spies was rampant in 1940. The Ministry of Information had set up an Anti-Gossip Committee, and many people were prosecuted under its powers.

On Saturday morning Mum, Diane and I went shopping in the village, leaving Jill at home with Gan. We joined an onion queue at the greengrocer's, behind Mrs Dewey. She turned to look at us.

"I don't know whether I dare speak to you, in case somebody is listening," she muttered. "If you ask me, there are a darn sight more English spies around than German ones."

"You sound as though someone's been getting at you." Mum was sympathetic and, without Gan to inhibit her, ready to chat. "What's up?"

"Not at me. It's my young brother-in-law. What do you think, someone has reported him for careless talk! I wouldn't care, but half the time our Sam wouldn't say a dicky-bird. He'd just be trying to impress his girlfriend, you know what lads are."

"What did he say?" Everybody in the queue shuffled forward a few steps nearer the shop.

"All he did was talk about one of the raids on Torpoint last week. I mean, everybody else in the cinema queue must have known about it."

"I don't know how they can call that careless talk," Mum said. "Not when it was common knowledge."

"No, and if he'd just left it at that, he might have got away with it. But the silly young beggar then went on to say what he thought the Germans were looking for."

"Well, but that was only speculation. How could that have helped any spy who was listening?"

Mrs Dewey's expression was becoming grim. "Because he *then* went on to say where they were."

"Where what were?"

"The oil tanks. And some sly b—in that queue reported him, so he's up before the magistrates next week."

Mum exclaimed, "Well, what a thing to accuse him of, when those oil tanks are so conspicuous, nobody could miss them!"

"You be careful," Mrs Dewey warned. "There might be someone behind you who'll report you for saying that."

"Oh, I'm sure . . ." A little flustered, Mum turned to look over her shoulder and encountered Mrs Dobson's twinkling black eyes.

"Don't you worry, me 'andsome," she chuckled, having obviously heard every word. "If anyone asks me who told where them Torpoint oil tanks are, I'll swear blind it wasn't you." As everyone laughed heartily, Mrs Dewey's glance fell on Diane and me, standing shyly behind Mum. "Have you left the little maid home with your mother?" she asked.

At Mum's nod she went on, "I've left our Effie looking after Pammie. She's got a bit of a sore throat, poor little maid. And what's this Effie's been telling me about your concert?" Her smile at Diane and me was kindly, but we instantly shot Mum a wary look.

"We haven't had a chance to tell Mum yet, because we don't see her all week," I said quickly. I didn't explain why we had not told Gan, which was simply because we had come to expect her to put a stop to anything we wanted to do.

We were encouraged at school to do all we could to help the war effort, and the latest craze among the children was to put on a concert in the Scouts' Hut behind the church. Every playtime for weeks, Diane and I, Effie Dewey, Eva Timble and Mary Penhallow had been practising a play, set around "Old King Cole". I do not know how we expected to keep it a secret from Gan for ever, but it was a relief now Mum knew. All she said was, "I hope it's on a Saturday, so I'll be able to come to it."

It was at this stage that everyone in the queue, from Mrs Dewey back to old Mrs Brown who had just joined it, realised they had something more serious to worry about than concerts and careless talk.

116

Mrs Dewey, glancing towards the counter, exclaimed, "Would you believe it, I think he's running out of onions."

There was a gasp of dismay all along the line, before hullabaloo broke out. Every woman in the queue protested, each in her own style. Mrs Dewey loudly gave her opinion of customers who had walked out with two pounds of onions while the rest were left with nothing, while Mrs Dobson, even more loudly, pronounced what she would like to do to shopkeepers who allowed such unfair practices. Mum only uttered little sighs of disappointment, while old Mrs Brown began to slide silently away.

Mr Smithson acted swiftly to quell the unrest. Calling Mrs Brown back, he addressed the queue. "Now then, ladies, I'm sorry I've run out. But if you'd all like to collect a chitty from the counter, you'll be first served when I get another load of onions. Now I can't say fairer than that, can I?"

Everyone was satisfied except Mrs Dobson. "Well, if my old man gives me hell, I'll send him round to you," she grumbled. "I promised him tripe and onions for his dinner. Now he'll have to settle for corned beef and carrots and he's not going to like it!"

On the way home, we told Mum all about our concert. "Leave it to me," she promised. "I'll see what I can sort out." Her words marked a turning point in my childhood. It was the first time I was aware of her taking our side, against Gan.

CHAPTER
FOURTEEN

'Diphtheria is Deadly. Protect Your Child.'
(*Government Poster*)

Mum's job made a tremendous difference to our family's finances. I can't recall it having much effect on our food, but then everybody was suffering shortages. I do remember Gan's sharp reprimand to me when, for the first time ever, the delicious smell of frying bacon hung in the room when Diane and I came down for our porridge.

"What is it?" I wondered.

"Bacon," Gan said shortly and when I joyfully asked whether we were going to have some, she snapped at me, "You are not. Bacon is for folks that work."

But if our food did not get any better, our entertainment did.

We had a wireless. As with other families as poor as we were, it was considered a necessity, coming after the rent and before food and clothes on our list of priorities. I expect that at times, it was the only thing that kept Mum and Gan sane. You could escape, with a wireless, into the humorous world of Bebe and Ben Lyon, or amongst ITMA's eccentric characters.

And of course, listening to the regular news bulletins was paramount. In the early months of the war, Mum and Gan had also listened to news from Germany. But when Lord Haw-Haw began his vindictive campaign of threats and boasts and they heard his gloating promise that 'Plymouth would be next', they stopped listening to him.

"If that snidey blighter thinks we're going to waste our battery just so he can put the wind up us, he's got another think coming," Gan declared. There had been times when we were unable to afford a battery for a while and when that happened, deep depression had engulfed all of us except Jill, though she, like the rest of us, suffered every time Gan's temper shortened. When Mum started work, that was one calamity which never befell us again. In addition, we began to go to the Forum cinema in Devonport.

There was a small cinema in the village, but since it was known locally as 'The Flea Pit', Mum and Gan would not go near it.

However, going to Devonport on the *Western Belle* was half the fun for us children, though Mum must have felt a little more blasé about it.

There were always long queues outside cinemas, but every shuffle forward took us closer to sheer bliss. Once inside the darkened hall, we eagerly drank in every magic minute of two full-length films and a news programme.

But it must have been hard for Jill, expected at three years old to sit still through over three hours of films which she could not have understood. Luckily she was a stoical little girl, taking most things without complaint. Sometimes she fell asleep in her seat. Other times, a bag of sweets helped. Mum had given each of us threepence a week from the day she brought home her first week's wages, and a halfpenny bought a lot of Dolly Mixtures or Tom Thumb drops. But Jill's real salvation lay in a bag of jam sandwiches with which she steadily munched her way through the long, tedious hours.

We also started going to seances in Devonport. Mum and Gan had often been disappointed at the Spiritualist Church, by not getting a 'message'. They found a medium's circle, where everyone was guaranteed one, on a payment of a small fee. You had to give the medium something personal to hold, which she slid in and out of her fingers before going into a trance.

On one occasion the medium began to speak in a deep, slow voice, quite unlike the one she had previously used.

"I see a fellow spirit," she intoned. "I feel the power of one who has healing hands."

We all shot uneasy glances at one another, all except Gan, who gazed steadily, and without surprise, at the medium.

"You have the gift, my dear, the power to see and the strength to heal." The medium paused, her eyes shut tight as she gazed into the spirit world. "I see a young woman, whose life you saved. Am I right?"

Gan answered the question. "Yes, that was Dorothy, my niece."

It was amazing. We all knew the story of Dorothy, Auntie Ida's daughter, who had nearly died of meningitis as a child, and whom Gan had always insisted she had saved by sleeping with her, willing her to live, when the illness was at its worst.

The medium nodded. "I can feel the strength that flowed from you to her. You must use it for others, my dear. And the gift of seeing — this also you must pass on."

We were hardly out of the front door of the terraced house, on the best, bay-windowed side of the street, before Gan's triumph erupted into words.

"Well, what about that?" she exclaimed to Mum as we started to walk to Ferry Street. "Wasn't that woman's reading uncanny! Of course I knew I had the gift of seeing, but healing . . . ! Though I always knew I'd saved Dorothy, even though your Uncle Claude wouldn't have it. Fancy, he had the nerve to say it was his mother's bread poultice that did it, but your Auntie Ida knew it was me. Well, I've said it before and I'll say it again. I've felt my strength grow since we joined the League. We have a lot to thank Sir Percy for."

It was the first time I had heard mention of Sir Percy since he had told Gan to tell me that George Washington was in his League, because he had been too brave to tell a lie. I knew quite well that Sir Percy was getting at me. Had he but known it, I was becoming as concerned about my own proclivity for distorting the truth as he was. For despite Miss Croft's assurances, prayers hadn't stopped it.

I even thought I had found a physical cure. When we started taking a newspaper and I began to get spending-money, I saw an advertisement for a toothpaste which, it was claimed, 'Stopped you telling white lies'. For weeks I secretly saved a penny a week to buy a tube of it, convinced that it would solve all my problems.

I was disillusioned long before I had saved enough money, but that brought its own problems. I had fourpence or fivepence burning a hole in my pocket so I spent it on a huge bag of Tom Thumb drops, Winter Mixtures and I don't know how many sherbet liquorices, and ate most of them in one glorious binge in the outside lavatory, the only place of complete privacy.

I got my just deserts though, for I made myself ill. Unable to tell Gan the truth, she thought I was sickening for something and I had to swallow a large dose of her remedy for all ills, the hated 'Ippycak'.

On our way home from Devonport, Sir Percy's high expectations of us were yet again brought to our notice.

122

As we climbed down the narrow gang-plank onto the *Western Belle*, the air-raid siren began to wail. The boatmen flung off the mooring ropes and jumped on as the boat swung round to head across the dark water to Southdown.

The skipper announced that he would keep going. "It'll be safer on our side anyway," he assured his passengers. As we sped across the wide expanse of the Tamar we could see searchlights begin to sweep the sky and then all the familiar noises of war began to sound off. The drones of planes got louder as they swept in from the sea, followed by the furious burst of anti-aircraft guns trying to bring them down. Behind us, we saw the flashes and heard the whistle of bombs as they fell onto Devonport.

Halfway across I whispered to Mum, sitting next to me with Jill on her knee, "What if a bomb drops on the boat? I can only see two lifebelts."

For one horrifying moment I was convinced Mum shared my alarm. She stared at me with her mouth open and clutched tighter to Jill. But Gan was made of sterner stuff.

"Don't you dare let Sir Percy hear you trying to frighten your little sister," she hissed, before Mum could say a word. "The boat is not going to be hit by a bomb, and if it was he'd expect members of the League to show a bit more gumption."

As she paused, I looked quickly at Jill, unconcernedly sucking her thumb. Gan's sibilant chiding continued, hushed so that other passengers would not hear. "And in that case, we'd sit Jill on that seat," I looked to where she was pointing, "which floats. We would all hold onto the handles and make sure she did not fall off. And now, let's hear no more about bombs dropping on us. Remember who you are!" Her words, uncompromising as usual, were also immediately comforting. I had not realised, until then, that the large, wooden-planked seats on the deck, hung around with rope-threaded handles, were buoyant.

It was not to be expected that Gan would neglect seizing the chance to try out her newly discovered healing skills on somebody. Unfortunately for me, I was the first to appear in need.

I came home from school one day with the glands behind my ears painfully swollen. "Let me feel," Gan commanded. When she ran her hands firmly over my sore neck, I flinched away from her.

"That hurts," I gasped.

"Then keep still, will you." Holding me by the nape she continued to press the sides of my neck where it hurt, while I continued to struggle. In a split second she lost her temper with me. One of her 'healing hands' flew off my neck, to land on my arm in a resounding slap.

I burst into tears. "Oh, for heaven's sake! If you're going to be mardy, I've done with you. And now look what you've done!"

Jill had begun to whimper in sympathy and Gan left me to hastily slap some jam onto a piece of bread.

"Here you are." She gave it to Jill, who obligingly stopped snuffling and began to eat, a solitary tear rolling down her cheek.

I think Gan must have felt sorry when I took to bed with mumps. Her voice gruff but unusually kind, she reproved me. "I could have stopped you getting this, if only you'd have let me. But you've got to have faith for it to work. Never mind, get this bread and milk down you, then off to sleep."

I was so unused to kind words from her that I fell asleep racked with guilt, knowing that somehow, my mumps served me right. But she suffered more than I did, with both Diane and Jill catching my germs over the next week or two.

Before I was well enough to return to school, three awful things happened concerning children we knew of, though not personally.

Mavis Penton, one of the older girls, had died after being taken to hospital with bad stomach pains. The rumour went round that she had died of twisted kidneys, brought on by doing handstands. Handstands, up against the school wall every playtime, had become a craze with all of us. I was always too clumsy to perform well, but Diane could do good, slow ones and stay up for ages. Mavis was one of the best. She could even do cartwheels all along the school path. However, her death, whatever the cause, brought a handstand ban on all of us.

The other tragedy was nearer home. Effie Dewey's older brother, David, who went to the boys' school at Four Lanes End, fell off the cliffs at Whitsands while collecting birds' eggs, and was killed. Everyone was shocked and upset for the Dewey family.

Gan, always deeply sympathetic when faced with real grief, went to see Mrs Dewey. She came back very subdued.

"That poor woman's at her wits' end," she said. "She blames herself for sending David off out of her way, what with her husband being on nights at the Dockyard and trying to sleep during the day, and Pammie sickening for something." Gan shook her head. "I didn't like the look of her, poor little mite. Nurse Johnson is expected round later today, but I'll take round some tincture of myrrh, to see if that will help."

In less than a week, three-year-old Pammie was dead from diphtheria. A row quickly developed over her burial which split the village in half.

There was a tremendous amount of sympathy for Mr and Mrs Dewey, after their double tragedy. So when they wanted to put up a wooden cross in the churchyard for Pammie, instead of stone or marble, and the vicar opposed it, all their neighbours rallied to them.

Mum was nearly in tears. "Mrs Dewey says they can't bear to think of Pammie with a cold stone cross," she faltered.

Gan cleared the emotion from her throat. "Who does that man think he is?" She had never liked the Rev. Webster. "Well, I never thought the day would come when I agreed with Mrs Dobson, but she's right. Somebody ought to shoot him!"

The vicar prevailed, but so did Mr and Mrs Dewey. Pammie lay in her little grave with no headstone, just a small bowl of flowers with her name on it.

Thinking about it now, I don't suppose the vicar had any choice in the materials to be used in his churchyard. But emotions ran so high in that sad winter of 1940, nobody was willing to give him the benefit of the doubt.

Then it was nearly Christmas and most families put aside their sorrows and worries and began to prepare for it.

Gan began a mammoth cooking session. She had already made the cake and puddings some weeks earlier, created from a thick, dark mix in her huge, cracked earthenware bowl. A third of the mixture was put into a cake-tin and baked in the range oven, and another third was divided up and put into three or four bits of old sheeting, boiled in the copper and then hung on nails in the wash-house to dry. The rest she put into old jam-jars and called it mincemeat.

Now, she brought out the jars and spooned their contents between thick rounds of pastry, into two rusty patty-tins. When they were cooked she gave us each a sample. They were more like highly-spiced Bakewell tarts than mince pies, but since we did not know the difference, we thought they were marvellous.

She made a trifle from stale biscuits, laced with some of her elderberry wine, and covered with a layer of custard, so solid that it had the consistency of rubber. And on Christmas Day, instead of boiling the rabbit, she roasted it, filling the house with its delicious smell.

The meal we sat down to enjoy seemed like a feast. Gan was flushed with her successes.

"And to think, if Mr Brown had got his way, you wouldn't have got this pudding," she insisted. "He was all for me tearing up all our old bits of cloth for bandages, in case of an emergency. But I told him the Christmas pudding had first claim. Well Ida," she raised her glass of elderberry wine. "Here's to a better Christmas than the last few. And Hitler didn't come either." The twenty-first of December had been hanging over us as a possible 'Invasion Date'. We all raised our glasses, Diane and I with our watered wine, and Jill with her elderberry-flavoured milk.

CHAPTER
FIFTEEN

'Turn your saucepans into Spitfires!'
(*Government Appeal for aluminium
from the Women of Britain*)

Mrs Timble came round on the first of January. "Happy New Year," she greeted us. "I can't stay long. I've left the kids squabbling over their comics."

Gan said jocularly, "We'd begun to think you'd fallen out with us," and Mrs Timble immediately took her literally.

"Oh no, Mrs Cooper," she assured Gan, looking quite distressed. "But I've been that busy, I've not known whether I was on my head or my heels. They've got me collecting recipes for a booklet to sell in the school bazaar." Mrs Timble could not hide her pride. "So I came to see if you have a favourite one you'd like me to put in."

"Of course. I've got several I can give you," Gan said grandly. "I'll write them out for you later. But have you time for a cup of tea first?"

Mrs Timble hadn't but allowed herself to be persuaded.

"So. What's the latest about Mrs Murdoch?" Gan poured two cups of dark walnut-coloured tea and settled down for a gossip.

"Well, did you hear about Mr Pendennis's ferret?"

Gan shook her head. "The last I heard, it was *Mrs* Pendennis telling me about having to have the bobby round again."

"Yes, well he's been round again, and all because Mr Pendennis's ferret got loose in the yard, and Mrs Murdoch shut herself upstairs and was screaming out of the window. It's a wonder you didn't hear her in West Street."

"Good Lord, that must have been some hullabaloo."

"You should have heard her! I think she thought it would climb up the wall and get her."

Mrs Timble's cackle of laughter trailed off at Gan's slightly disapproving expression. "Well, poor woman, she was probably genuinely frightened. I must admit, I don't like ferrets myself."

Mrs Timble gulped. "That's just what I said, Mrs Cooper. The poor old dear was most likely scared stiff."

"Mind you," Gan became thoughtful, "we can't expect people to put up with disturbance of the peace, just because of one daft woman."

"You're so right, Mrs Cooper. She ought to be put away."

"But I suppose we all have to be more tolerant, when none of us knows what's ahead of us. It's up to us all to help one another."

By the time the two women had talked and drunk tea for half an hour, it was hard to tell what Mrs Timble's true opinions were, except that they were the same as Gan's. When she had gone, Gan had a look at the tea-leaves left in her visitor's cup.

"Just look at that!" she exclaimed. "A woman with clouds around her. That means jealousy. I *thought* she didn't look too keen when I mentioned my recipes. I bet she thought I wouldn't have one."

Mrs Timble wasn't the only woman doing her bit for the war effort. Everyone, particularly the women and children, helped in every way they could. Much of their efforts involved the collection of salvage and we were often told exactly what it would be used for, which added another dimension to our enthusiasm. But though Gan was as patriotic as any of them, she often had to put our personal needs before national ones.

Very early in the war, an appeal was made to women to give up their aluminium pots and pans, so they could be made into Spitfires and Wellington bombers. Gan was mortified because she only had one large pan made of aluminium, and that was the one in which she stewed the rabbits. Twice, when the WVS lady called for donations, Gan hissed at us to keep away from the window, refusing to answer the door.

The pigs never received our potato peelings and leftovers either, because she used peelings to help keep the fire going, and made any leftovers into bubble and squeak or rissoles.

My salvage collection was raided before it ever reached Miss Croft. Gan used newspaper instead of a tablecloth and hung smaller pieces on a string in the lavatory. She cut out cardboard soles and saved them to keep our feet temporarily dry, when our shoes were letting in the wet.

She did have the satisfaction of saving tins, to be reconstructed into tanks. But her enthusiasm for saving rabbit bones for a 'bones into glue' bin, which Mr Dobson collected once a week, was marred by Mrs Dobson's jest, when she saw Gan emptying them in.

"Well, that poor little thing won't stick many aeroplanes' wings on," she chuckled, not really unkindly. But Mrs Pendennis was just being ushered out of the house opposite by old Mrs Brown, and Gan was put out at the titters of the two ladies. Her normal powers of riposte for once failed her.

But if the joys of filling all the salvage receptacles were denied her, Gan relished what she saw as her role of comforter to women whose men were away. Mrs Timble, Mrs Finchcombe and Tilda were all encouraged when they wanted to talk about their absent menfolk, and urged to when they did not. Mrs Timble and Tilda, with their children, had open invitations to come to us if they were nervous in a night raid. Since we only had two bedrooms, with one double bed in each, I don't know what we would have done if they had all turned up at once.

But it was a different matter when the vicar expressed much the same sentiments as Gan about women's loyalty to their men.

The Rev. Webster caused another stir when he preached a sermon about the morals of some women in the village whose husbands were away. Of course he did not name anyone, but Gan reckoned she knew who he meant. Like other women, she was indignant.

"It'd serve him right if someone sued him," she declared. "Fancy saying something like that, which will upset the men at the Front if they hear about it."

I asked, "What are the sins of the flesh?"

She snapped back at me, "Something you're too young to be asking about." And I was none the wiser for being able to interpret her cryptic aside to Mum, "At-th ittle-l adam-M will be ucky-l if some usybody-b doesn't ite-wr and ell-t her husband. Well, I've ied-tr all I an-c. It's up to her."

Gan had strong opinions about men's and women's roles in life, which Mum very occasionally disagreed with. They did not see eye to eye on Tilda Hawkins, for instance. Tilda was very pretty and seemed well-dressed compared to many of the young village women.

Gan came back from the Post Office one day, very disapproving. "I've just seen Tilda Hawkins. She was laid out like lamb and lettuce. I'm not kidding, you'd have thought she was dressed for a wedding."

Mum said gently, "Well, why shouldn't she dress nicely if she can afford to?"

"Because that's the point. How does she afford to?"

"She'll get an Army allowance from Greg. I'm sure he'd want her to be nicely dressed."

"Oh no, he wouldn't. Not if he'd seen her today."

"Oh, Mum! What do you expect her to do? Go round dressed like a nun, just because her husband is away?"

"I'd think a damn sight better of her if she did." Gan then pronounced in portentous tones, "Men must fight and women must weep!"

"Oh, for heaven's sake, Mum. And it's 'work' not 'fight'!" We had never heard Mum's voice raised to Gan, who was obviously as shocked as we were.

"In wartime, it's 'fight'. And don't you take that tone with me, my girl."

They quickly became aware of three anxious pairs of eyes watching them. We had never heard them row before, only Gan being nasty and Mum taking it.

Gan quickly recovered herself enough to snap at Diane and me, "You two, go and feed the cat. Why should I always have to do it?"

I began to scuttle for the door without a word. Diane stayed to ask a sensible question and got her head bitten off for it.

"What's he having?"

"Just go and find him first. I must have been mad to ever let you have a cat, *I'm* always the one who has to look after it."

Diane hastened to join me, as fearful as I suddenly was that Gan, in a fit of temper, would get rid of Winkle.

PC Polworthy, had he but known it, stirred up another difference between Mum and Gan. He was very critical of a decision to recruit three women to the ranks of the Cornish Police Force for the duration of the war, and held forth on the subject with sympathetic listeners. Gan was one of them.

"You know, he's right, Ida," she said. "Women should never be allowed to take over jobs meant for men."

Mum said, "Why ever not?"

It was a Sunday afternoon and we were setting off for our walk.

"Why not? Because it's asking for trouble, that's why not."

"What about me? I do a man's job."

There was an ominous pause. Diane and I looked at one another. It sounded like another fall-out.

But we were wrong. As we approached the bottom of Donkey Lane, Gan found a surer way than arguing, to assert her authority. "That's different and you know it. You do a man's job because you haven't got one to do it for you. Anyway," her tone announced the end of the discussion, "let's go this way. We haven't been for a while!" With heavy hearts we obediently set off in the direction of Wiggle Farm.

That walk past the belligerent geese followed the same pattern as all the others. The geese terrified all of us except Gan, who was loud in her contempt of anyone who showed their fear.

"They know when you're afraid of them." She tried to stiffen my backbone. "Stare them out."

But it was me who was stared out, by a particularly huge bird which I suppose could have been the gander. It fixed me with a knowing eye, before starting its neck-forward sprint towards me.

Not even Gan's exhortations could keep me facing it, and I gave Sir Percy no chance to get his oar in. I shot round the other side of Diane, at her usual place hanging on to Jill's push-chair handle, only too thankful to exchange the bird's hostility for Gan's.

Gan got her comeuppance over those geese, though I did not appreciate the irony of it until I was much older.

She had an unkind way of trying to shame me out of my sins, by extolling Diane's virtues. "Diane wouldn't tell fibs," she would scorn. I knew it was true. "And she's younger than you."

"You're older than Diane, you shouldn't need help to get dressed," she sternly reminded me, when I wasn't quick enough pulling my clothes on at the onset of a night raid.

One day, on the way to Wiggle Farm, she pushed me away when I began to walk beside her. "You go and hold onto the pram," she sneered. "Diane will be brave and walk with me."

Poor Diane. She didn't want to be brave any more than I did. From my comparative safety on the far side of the push-chair, I saw her panic as the geese rushed out to meet us.

Gan's appeals to her courage, her warnings over the lack of it, were as unavailing with my sister as they had been with me. She was too frightened to hear.

"Face them! Don't run, Diane, they'll only run after you."

But Diane ran, as fast as she could, for the push-chair, leaving Gan to stand her ground.

Gan glared into the baleful eye of the leader of the flock, obviously expecting to subdue it. But she didn't. With an angry hiss, it dived at her leg, sinking its strong beak through her thick lisle stocking.

If her firm stare hadn't stopped the geese in their tracks, her shriek did, at least for long enough to allow her to join us at top speed.

At the end of the lane out of sight of the farm, when we all stopped for breath, Mum tried to offer sympathy. "Shall I tie my hanky round it," she offered.

"No," Gan answered, tight-lipped. "It'll do till we get home. And I'll tell you something else while I'm at it. That's the last time I try to put a bit of backbone into your kids."

Of course it wasn't, but she did give up over the geese.

CHAPTER
SIXTEEN

'If fighting breaks out in your neighbourhood —
Stand Firm!'
(*Government Pamphlet* —
'*Beating the Invader*' — *Spring 1941*)

We became ever more enthusiastic at school, raising money for the war effort. In addition to the usual raffles and bazaars, concerts and competitions, many children got together in small groups and put on their own plays, to which they invited all their friends and relations at threepence each.

Diane and I and half-a-dozen other girls had settled on a jazzed-up version of "Old King Cole" as our offering, and to our relief, thanks to Mum's behind-the-scenes cajolery, Gan became agreeably interested in it. I was delighted, at first, to get the title part, though I knew it was only because I was the tallest. The rest of the parts were handed out for equally practical reasons.

Diane was the Dancing Fairy. Both she and Sally Finton had practised the role. Diane was a dainty little girl, light on her feet, while Sally was nearly as tall as me, and quite a lot wider. But Diane's clinching advantage came only when Gan said she could borrow a pure silk, embroidered shawl with a long, dangling

139

fringe, laid by in tissue paper from better days. So Sally reluctantly settled for Second Fiddler.

Mary Penhallow had the promise of her cousin's bridesmaid's dress, so she was the obvious choice for Young Queen Cole, while Avril Smith was asked to join us because she was the smallest girl in Diane's class, ideal for the Child.

Eva Timble had been going to singing lessons. She had a nice voice and was very willing to use it. So she sang the rhyme at regular intervals, with one or two songs of her own repertoire thrown in.

Effie Dewey, her noisy, extrovert character subdued since losing her brother and little sister, had been chosen as the main Fiddler because her Uncle had agreed she could borrow his banjo. Effie had talked of dropping out, until her dad said she must go on doing her best to help win the war. With the other two girls as the second and third Fiddlers, equipped with cardboard fiddles, we were ready to do our bit.

With one exception, our play was an utter fiasco. The main reason was the staggeringly large audience we attracted, and a good percentage of them were rowdy boys from Four Lanes End school. With well over a hundred and fifty in the Scouts' hall, and no adult in charge, they took over and our earnest little play became a butt for boisterous laughter.

We had made matters worse by starting all over again when we saw Mum, Gan, Jill and Mrs Timble make a late arrival. The result was as hard on them as on us, since they had to find their seats amidst a barrage of whistles and feet-stamping.

I was wearing navy-blue bloomers stuffed with cushions, which were so heavy they fell down. Mary Penhallow's piping little voice could not be heard above the audience's hilarity, while Avril went one better than the proverbial Victorian child. She was neither seen nor heard.

Diane flitted gracefully across the floor, her arms waving the long strands of her shawl up and down, while her wand wafted nervously, nineteen to the dozen. Effie and her fellow Fiddlers stood manfully at the back of the stage, frantically fiddling to Eva Timble's brave warbling.

Eva had the only moment of triumph. As we thankfully neared the end of our performance, she broke into her star turn of *Jerusalem*, and the noisy audience was taken by surprise. For a few minutes they actually listened and we all reaped the advantage as we came to the front of the stage to bow.

I don't know who suffered the most, Mum and Gan or us. And Gan had been even more incensed by Mrs Timble's complacency.

"Would you credit it?" Gan fumed, as we made our subdued way home. "When I had the grace to praise her kid's voice, she couldn't find one good word to say about ours."

"She was just jealous," Mum said stoutly, glancing at Diane's and my abashed expressions.

"I don't know about jealous, but she's as dense as they come. Watch what you're doing, will you!" Gan added an irritable aside to me when I dropped a cushion. "Would you believe it, when I told her everybody got a shock to hear *Jerusalem* in the middle of "Old King Cole", she took it as a compliment. 'Yes, Mrs Cooper,' " Gan simpered in mock imitation of Mrs Timble. " 'You're so right. I think the last thing they expected was to hear a voice like my Eva's.' " She snorted in disgust. "Well she's the first woman I've ever come across, who doesn't know when she's being put down."

A complete fiasco, but with one exception. With one hundred and seventy-four tickets sold at the door, we made two pounds three shillings and sixpence for the war effort. And no matter how little we had been appreciated, no one had the nerve to ask for their money back.

I must have been the eternal optimist, or daft. There was a singing competition at school, with a fifteen shilling Savings Certificate for First Prize, and Savings Stamps of ten shillings and five shillings for second and third prizes. I asked Gan if I could enter it. "Eva Timble is going to," I told her. "She's singing *Jerusalem*."

I thought Gan was going to explode. "No you can't," the words burst from her.

"But why not? Eva Timble . . ."

"If you mention *Jerusalem* once more, I'll crown you!"

I gabbled a hasty denial. "I wasn't going to. Miss Croft says I could sing *Early One Morning*."

"Oh, does she! Well, you can tell her from me . . ." My heart had dropped to my boots, before the final words were out of her mouth. "*We'll* decide what you can or can't do."

142

I badly wanted to go in for that competition, otherwise I would never have persisted against her. "So, can I?"

"No."

"But why?"

Gan shot out a once-and-for-all, exasperated retort, which silenced all argument. "Because you'd come second," she snapped, "and that's the end of it."

I was bitterly disappointed. Singing was a strong element in our school life. I loved it, though the songs I remember now all seem to tell of woman's sad lot in life. "Oh don't deceive me," we trilled. "Oh never leave me. How could you use a poor maiden so?"

Although most of the air-raids were now in the early evening or at night, we did still get daylight raids which affected school life.

Our teachers were adamant that they should not stop us learning.

So we had "Shelter work" always ready, to snatch up with our gas-masks as soon as the siren sounded. We learned our tables and recitations in the shelter, and were ruthlessly tested on them when the raid was over.

My relationship with Miss Croft got closer as I began to see more of her. She held knitting and sewing circles in her house after school, inviting half-a-dozen girls of which I was often one. I loved going there. Although she was kind to all of us, I knew she had a special interest in me. I knew why too. It was because I was a sinner to be saved, but I didn't mind. At a time when I felt of such little account at home, the idea that someone actually thought I was worth saving was wonderful. But I had learned my lesson, and kept secret the strong religious beliefs she was instilling into me.

Poor Miss Croft was dealt a disappointing blow that winter. Her reputation for filling her home with bundles of cloth for children's nighties, and skeins of wool for refugee blankets, milk bottle tops and old rubber soles and heels, but most of all, huge stacks of newspapers, became her downfall. Her landlord gave her notice to quit, for making his house a fire hazard.

"One incendiary, and the whole damn lot will go up," he insisted and she had to settle for a smaller house in another street, where presumably the landlord was more patriotic.

In February that year there was another invasion warning and many people really expected to see the sky thick with parachutes, the sea full of landing-craft. All except Gan.

"How many times has Hitler said he was coming, then didn't?" she scornfully asked. "He's just trying to put the wind up us."

But the Government took the threat seriously and in the spring of 1941 issued another Invasion Pamphlet. I never got to know all it contained, only the bits that annoyed Gan.

Her main irritation was over the powers to be given to the Civil Defence services in general, and to Mr Brown in particular.

There was a knock on the door one day, just as Diane, Jill and I had started our evening meal. Gan had hers later, when Mum came home from work. It was not the usual Monday bubble-and-squeak. Diane and I each got two large, thick rounds of something well browned, and Jill got one round.

It was always asking for trouble to question Gan about her gastronomic offerings. She invariably took it personally, as though she expected us to grumble, yet we never did. Diane was the only one with the guts to ask, "What are they?"

"They're rissoles," Gan barked at her. "Get them down you."

The knock on the door diverted her and she darted to the window to see who it was.

"It's Mrs Pendennis," she sighed. "I'll have to answer it. She knows we're in. You get on with your meal."

Mrs Pendennis came in with a cup of sugar. "Mrs Brown asked me to bring it over," she said. "Poor soul, she's stiff with her rheumatics."

The obligatory cup of tea was offered, as always, despite rationing. Gan had started adding a dried, dark green substance to her caddy, to make the ration go further, but she never admitted to what it was. It did not matter to me, because I had long given up tea for water, but Mrs Pendennis pulled a wry face.

"My, you make a good, strong cup of tea, Mrs Cooper. This should put a lining on our stomachs."

Gan took her comment as a compliment. Perhaps it was. "The secret's in the brewing," she claimed. "I give it twice as long as they say." In fact, it was more like ten times as long, with the large brown teapot added to but never emptied, from morning till night.

"So poor old Mrs Brown has rheumatism? And what does she think of her hubby's duties if we get invaded?"

"She doesn't think much of them, I can tell you."
Mrs Pendennis put down her cup, ready for a
gossip. "And as for that bit about no Civil Defence
people being allowed to lie low if the Germans invade
their village . . . Mrs Brown says she will have
something to say to that. I mean, what could her old
man do?"

Mrs Pendennis's chins began to quiver. "He
wouldn't hear them coming, for a start."

Gan chortled in agreement, but revealed what really
peeved her. "And as for taking orders from him . . . it's
ridiculous. I don't mind taking them from PC
Polworthy, or the Army, but not Mr Brown. Why, the
number of times he gets the wrong end of the stick,
he'd be telling us to lie low, when he should be saying,
'Stand firm'."

Gan and Mrs Pendennis shared the same taste in humour. As they carried on ridiculing poor Mr Brown, though never with any real cruelty, we concentrated on our rissoles. Apart from their shape and some added carrot, they tasted just the same as bubble-and-squeak. We hungrily ploughed our way through them.

Mrs Pendennis was taking her leave. Heaving herself out of her chair, she cast an interested glance at our plates. "That almost looks good enough to eat," she joked.

"Well, I don't need to give you the recipe," Gan said, apparently not noticing that Mrs Pendennis had not asked for it. "It's a Ministry of Food rissole recipe that I've adapted. You just put anything you've got into them, as long as it fries, with a spoonful of milk to bind it. The kids love them."

Her eyes challenged us. She need not have worried about Jill and me. We were always hungry enough to eat anything. Diane did not have such a robust appetite, but she did have enough sense not to contradict.

CHAPTER
SEVENTEEN

'The weariest nights, the longest
days, sooner or later must
perforce come to an end.'
(*The Scarlet Pimpernel by Baroness Orczy*)

Although we were always in bed before Mum came
home, we were seldom asleep. She got into the habit of
coming up to say goodnight, while Gan was putting
their meal out.

One night she sat on our bed and told us, "Guess
what! The King and Queen were in Plymouth today."

"Oh, Mum!" Both Diane and I were thrilled. "Did
you see them?"

Mum shook her head. "No," she sighed. "We didn't
know they were here until after we were back for
the afternoon shift. The mother of one of the girls saw
them though. She says everyone was cheering like
mad."

"Perhaps you'll see them tomorrow, Mum."

"No. They were going back on the train to London,
later in the afternoon." She got up from our bed as
Gan's impatient voice wafted up the stairs.

"It's on the table, Ida."

"Off you go to sleep, there's good girls." She kissed
us and went down for her meal.

We were still not asleep when the siren started. Under the rag-rug I was keeping Diane and myself awake with another instalment of the latest product of my vivid imagination.

The stories I made up, to beguile the long, boring hours before we were ready for sleep, owed much to what I was reading at the time. Mum and Gan had a lot of books, picked up from secondhand shops. Besides most of Baroness Orczy's tales of the French Revolution, they included Georgette Heyer's Regency romances and Conan Doyle's detective stories. As soon as I could read I delved into them, filling myself with these grown-up tales long before I came across such children's classics as *Treasure Island* and *Ivanhoe* at school.

So *These Old Shades* inspired a nightly chase and escape, involving a wicked French Comte and two little English girls, which lasted a full week before the villain got his just desserts.

And the *Speckled Band*? That turned into such a lurid tale of snakes slithering into the bed of two sleeping children, I gave myself a nightmare. Waking in the night, sweating and shrieking, I frightened both Diane and Jill.

Mum and Gan were furious with me . . . well, Gan was furious, Mum was annoyed. "This is what comes of reading books too old for you," Gan fumed, and Conan Doyle was banned.

Diane and I lay still, despite the siren. It wasn't late, because Mum and Gan hadn't yet come to bed. Then, as the drone of aircraft became louder overhead, followed by the usual angry barrage from the cliff-top gun-sites, PC Polworthy blew his whistle, urgency in the sudden, prolonged shrill blasts, and Mum and Gan came rushing upstairs.

"It's a big one," Gan said briefly. "Get dressed quickly, Betty." She snatched up a jumper and dragged it over Diane's head, while Mum went to get Jill.

We hurried downstairs to the wash-house. As we huddled together against the outer wall, wave after wave of bombers flew over the village. As one wave headed for Plymouth, another followed it, so that the time that we cowered, waiting for them to pass, seemed never-ending.

The walls of the wash-house were thin, not being an integral part of the house. The deafening noise woke Jill from her cosy cocoon inside Mum's cardigan. She stared round at us all, her eyes full of sleep but her mouth beginning to tremble.

"There, there, my love, it's all right," Mum crooned to her, but we could hear the quiver in her voice.

Gan suddenly ordered, "Recite *Lochinvar*, Betty." So as the Germans were taking their incendiaries and high explosives to drop on Plymouth and Devonport, I obediently went through *Lochinvar, Sir Richard Grenville's Last Fight, The Noble Boy*, and I don't know how many others of my considerable repertoire of poems, all having the advantage of being long. Gan hardly let me recover breath after one, before insisting on another.

She did make Diane contribute, but since Diane seldom got beyond the first verse of her poems, it was soon back to me and another rendering of *Lochinvar*.

As I finished the last line for the second time, Gan said, "There, listen."

We listened. "They've passed," she said. "We're all right now, though poor old Plymouth is getting it again. And you know why they've come tonight, Ida? They think the King and Queen are still here, the swine. To think that there must be a spy somewhere, who let them know of the Royal visit. Well, I hope whoever it was has got one of their own bombs dropped on them."

The planes might have passed, but we could now hear explosions added to the din caused by our own guns. Gan announced, in her not-to-be-argued-with voice, "I'm going up the garden, to see what's happening."

"Mum, for heaven's sake, don't." Mum's voice was sharp. "It's too risky."

"Don't worry, I'll be back down before they come back."

"If PC Polworthy sees you, you'll be in trouble."

For a moment Gan hesitated, before confidently asserting, "He'll have enough on his hands tonight, without bothering about me."

She came back quicker than we expected. "I don't know about German bombs, but a bit of our own shrapnel's just missed me," she told us grimly.

She sat beside Mum, ignoring her exclamation of alarm. "They'll be coming back soon," she said, her voice gruff with emotion. "They're dropping flares over Plymouth, bright red, blue and green lights, to show them where to drop their bombs. And there are fire glows over Plymouth and Devonport. I'm sure the dockyard's been hit too. There are fires blazing near the water's edge."

She looked at Diane's and my weary faces. "Keep your chins up," she commanded. "You don't want Sir Percy to think you're windy, do you?"

"No," we dutifully agreed. But we were really too tired to care.

We were almost asleep when the planes began to come back, for the raid lasted far longer than Gan had envisaged. As we woke to their flight back to the sea, stiff from our uncomfortable positions on the rug, leaning against Mum's and Gan's knees, Gan began to carry on her usual running commentary.

"There's a lot less of them. And you can tell some of them have been hit. Can you hear that high-pitched whine?" We could; it sounded like a diving plane but she insisted, "That's a damaged aircraft. It won't make it back across the Channel." And when, soon after, we heard a tremendous explosion from the direction of Rame Head, she immediately claimed in triumph, "There, I told you!"

I can't remember how we got back to bed that night, but we overslept the following morning. Poor Mum, though, had to be at the Dockyard at the usual time. We, like other children, were sent to school as usual, though many fell asleep at their desks before the day was out.

There was a worse raid the following night. It started at nine o'clock, then was followed by another at two-thirty in the morning.

Then came a succession of long, weary nights, in which bouts of uneasy sleep and uneasier wakefulness alternated. We started going to bed dressed, to save precious minutes in our nightly dash for the wash-house.

Gan began to leave a tray of food ready for us, to keep off night starvation, she said. So in between my endless recitations, we munched our way through thick jam and cream-cracker sandwiches and Mum and Gan swallowed countless cups of tea.

Though we were all worn out, we went to Devonport the following Saturday afternoon, wondering if the Forum would still be there. It was, with a great long queue standing in the rubble of Devonport's main street, waiting to go in. Further down the street, we could see only Marks and Spencer still standing. Mrs Reuben's second-hand shop had gone, where most of our clothes had been bought in the days before Mum got her job.

Those half-dozen or so raids in the spring of 1941, when many of the Cornish border farms and villages were hit, and Plymouth and Devonport laid to waste, now merge in my mind into one long-drawn-out, incredibly noisy episode in our lives, when we seemed to spend whole nights stumbling in and out of bed. Often, bombers came back when we thought they had gone home. Gan began to misread the signals, though she never admitted it. "That's them on their way out," she insisted, when it was another lot coming in.

Mrs Timble came knocking on our door, the morning after a bad raid. "Oh, Mrs Cooper," she began. "Did you mean it, about coming to you if . . . if the kids were scared? They were terrified last night."

"Of course I did." Gan immediately reassured her. "Come in."

Eva Timble was with her mother. She, Diane and I set off for school. "We're coming to sleep with you tonight," Eva told us.

We were thrilled. That night, Diane and I were put in at the foot of Mum's and Gan's bed, to free ours for Mrs Timble and Eva. A bed was made for Jill in a drawer from the chest and her cot put in the other room, for three-year-old Garry.

The Timbles arrived with their blankets at about eight o'clock. Jill was asleep, dressed in her leggings and a jumper, her hard bed made comfortable with a layer of Mum's woollies beneath her.

Diane and I were also fully dressed, except for our shoes. Heaven knows what a mess we must have looked at school the next day.

We heard Gan and Mrs Timble bringing Eva and the bedding up the steep stairs. "Ssssshhh," Gan whispered. "Our kids are always asleep well before seven." It was more often after nine before we slept, but we would never have dared to contradict her.

Those first nights the Timbles spent with us were exhilarating. We all drew courage from being with outsiders. Somehow, things didn't seem so frightening with so many of us crowded together in our tiny wash-house. Mrs Timble brought cold potato patties to augment Gan's jam sandwiches, and the three women shared innumerable cups of tea.

And we had plenty of entertainment. When I wasn't reciting *Lochinvar*, or my latest marathon effort, *The Lady of Shalot*, Eva was singing. She sang *Jerusalem* at Gan's special request, with an encore when Mum added her praise. But she knew other songs too, and she and I joined in duets of our school songs. We sang so plaintively of sad Mary's plea not to be deceived and deserted, and poor Polly's cry, 'Take pity upon me, unfortunate maid!' we brought tears to my eyes if to no one else's. I was going through a very over-emotional stage, easily stirred to tears by a sad song or story.

Gan, with her robust, no-nonsense attitude to life, must have found me exasperating. It was no wonder that she brusquely told me to "Stop being so mardy," and started us off on a spirited rendering of *Roll out the Barrel*.

155

One night, Winkle, the cat hadn't come home. I looked for him all the following morning until it was time to go to school, and again at lunch-time. That evening, after our meal, I searched the garden again and found him hiding in the outside lavatory.

I could see his eyes glittering at me in the dim light, as he cowered at the side of the lavatory. As I bent to pick him up he sprang at me, his claws missing my face but giving me a nasty scratch on my hand. I knew something was wrong. He was usually such a gentle little cat.

Tilda was out in her backyard and heard me yell. "Are you all right, Betty?" she called.

"It's the cat. He's just scratched me."

By this time, Gan and Diane had come out. Gan went to look at Winkle, and she got pounced on too, though he still refused to come out of his dark little refuge.

"I think he's having a fit," she told us, closing the door on him. "Keep out of there until I get someone to see to him." She looked across at Tilda and said humorously, "This is where we could do with a man, Tilda."

"Well, as it happens . . ." Tilda moved to her door and called, "George? Can you come here a minute?"

She looked at Gan with a little smile. "It's lucky George Dorman happens to be here, Mrs Cooper. He's just called in to tell me about the bombs dropped at Southdown last night. One of them breached the sea-wall, and George and half-a-dozen others spent half the night repairing it before the next high tide."

I'd never seen George Dorman before and was very impressed as the tall, well-built man emerged from Tilda's kitchen. This was one of the men who had captured the German prisoners. Gan didn't look impressed though. She was staring at George with one of her most disapproving expressions and speaking in a tone calculated to flatten.

"I wouldn't dream of troubling Mr Dorman," she began, before George cheerfully interrupted.

"No bother, Mrs Cooper," he insisted. "It can't be left there, to hurt these two little maids. Have you got an old sack, or a piece of strong cloth?"

"I'm afraid . . ."

"I have, George. Wait a minute." Tilda dashed inside and came out with a potato sack. "Will this do?"

"Just the job. I'll come round over the garden wall, Mrs Cooper."

We didn't see any more, only Gan's icy face as she sent Diane and me inside. She was in no mood to be kind when she came in.

"What's going to happen to Winkle?" I asked anxiously, and received her short, uncompromising answer. "George Dorman is going to drown him."

I felt sick at the sudden rush of anxiety to my stomach. "But why? What . . . what's the matter with him?"

"Because he's having fits. He must have been frightened to death being out in that raid last night. Oh, don't you start!" Tears had begun to pour down my face. "I've had more than enough to put up with this morning. And let me have a look at that scratch."

She looked at my hand then got a piece of clean rag from the cupboard and put it in a bowl, before pouring boiling water over it. I knew I was in for some germ-killing. Sobs which I couldn't control shook me but even when the hot poultice was pressed on the scratch, I was crying more for poor Winkle than my scalding hand.

Gradually, Gan began to cool off the Timbles. We were all very sensitive to her moods, her likes and dislikes. After she had grumbled about Mrs Timble always bringing potato patties and never bringing tea and complained of her children's behaviour, we knew that her welcome mat was beginning to wear out.

One morning, when I was having a quick, cold wash in the stone sink, around three empty teacups, Gan came storming in.

"You've not mixed those cups up, have you?" she reproached. "I wanted to read Madam Timble's." That was another bad sign, when she called someone "Madam".

"No," I hastily lied. "They're just the same. I only pushed them back a bit."

"So you didn't move this one on the left?" She picked it up and glared accusingly at me.

"No." I shook my head and backed away, grabbing at the towel. "It's just where it was."

Gan looked long and hard into the cup, then said in a satisfied voice, "Just as I thought. There's trouble in *her* tea-leaves and she'll bring it on herself. Her cup's a mass of twisted lines, right near the top. Look, can you see?"

I obediently looked and didn't see, but said I did. Gan didn't usually discuss her tea-leaves readings with me but I suppose this instance was merely another excuse to say something derogatory about Mrs Timble. "That means a loss, fairly soon, and it's something to do with another woman. Well, I'm not warning her this time. Let her find out for herself!"

I escaped into the kitchen. I never doubted Gan's skill in reading the tea-leaves. But since I had shifted all the cups out of range of the tap, when my face flannel had fallen into one of them, I did wonder which one she had read. Mrs Timble's or Mum's? Or her own?

CHAPTER
EIGHTEEN

'Watch out for the toad-in-the-hole.
It could be sprouts-in-the-spuds, in disguise.'

After a series of niggling complaints about the Timble family, Gan found a serious one. It came in the form of a bug, which she found in the flock mattress on the bed Diane and I normally shared.

She was genuinely horrified. We all were. Although we got regular doses of nits in our hair, like many of the schoolchildren, and we certainly brought home fleas on occasions, because I can remember seeing Gan catch them, we had never seen a bug before.

Gan was all for confronting Mrs Timble with it . . . she had it in a matchbox . . . but Mum managed to dissuade her.

"For heaven's sake, Mum! We don't *know* that she brought it."

Gan was furiously indignant. "Well, who do you think did? Me?"

"Of course not, Mum. It's just as likely to be the kids. Or me. You never know who you're brushing up against. It could have come from anywhere."

"And I tell you, it didn't. That woman brought it. When I think of all those blasted cold potato cakes and having to listen to that kid's squeaky voice night after night . . . and then she lands us with a bug!"

Mum unhappily agreed. "I'm sure you're right and it was her. But it's not something you can go rushing round accusing people of. She'd be mortified."

"And I should jolly well hope she would be. So what do you suggest we do? Invite her to come back and bring us another?"

The difference between them was rapidly degenerating into a first-class row. And they'd obviously forgotten we three children were there, taking it all in. We didn't often hear Mum and Gan quarrel, because Mum usually gave way first. This time, she was uncharacteristically adamant that Gan should give the Timble family the benefit of doubt.

However, she did try to appease. "They probably won't be coming for much longer," she soothed. "It looks as though the raids might be easing off. We didn't have one last night, did we? Can't you get something that would kill bugs?"

Gan gave in with a bad grace. "I suppose I could smother the mattress with Keating's Powder," she reluctantly agreed. "But how I'm going to keep a still tongue in my head when I see Madam Timble again, I don't know."

That she did keep a still tongue in her head probably intimidated Mrs Timble just as much as a full-scale quarrel. Gan in one of her coldly aloof moods could put a damper on anyone's spirits. The Timbles slept at our house for one more raid, then didn't come again. Though there had been no actual fall-out, it must have been clear they had outstayed their welcome.

After a few nights, respite, the raiders came back in force, in the second half of April, 1941. Everywhere, we saw signs of the terrible destruction wreaked on Plymouth and everyone in the vicinity.

Plymouth was on fire. Devonport Dockyard was badly damaged. Mum was very upset when a man working on the next drilling machine to hers was killed on the night shift. He was one of many.

The small towns of Torpoint and Saltash were attacked. Forty houses were burned down in Saltash while at Torpoint the Oil Depot was hit, so that flames, then thick black smoke could be seen for miles, pouring from the huge tanks.

We got first-hand news of Torpoint from Mrs Finchcombe. Her daughter was bombed out, luckily with no injuries to her family, and she and her children came to stay in the Finchcombe's tiny cottage. Iris's

162

husband was at the Naval Camp on the outskirts of Torpoint, also unhurt, though forty-three sailors were killed there that night.

Despite the bombing of Saltash and Torpoint, they received an exodus of bombed-out people from Plymouth and Devonport. They packed the ferries each night, with their bundles of bedding and food, and those who could not find or afford accommodation made for the fields outside the towns, and slept in the hedges.

We went to Plymouth on a Saturday afternoon at the end of that month. Most of the shops in the city centre had disappeared, to be replaced by food stalls, a huge open-air market which was erected each morning, dismantled each night.

On our way home through Devonport we went to a Spiritualist Church. I can't remember whether we got a message on that occasion, but vividly recall the atmosphere in that crowded room. People were sombre, many anxious. The prayers said at the end of the service seemed to have a deep significance. The medium prayed that we would all come safely through the night and we sang *Abide with Me*. It made such an impression on me, that I can still remember the tone of her voice.

We made our way back to the quay through what was left of Devonport. But the Forum was still there, and a few shops. One had a notice in the window: 'If there is a Fire please get the paraffin out and the cat. Owner has gone to the country.'

In another was a long list:

No herrings, kippers or sprats, smoked or plain.
No fish of any sort.
No sultanas, currants or raisins.
No matches or firewood.
No fat or dripping.
No tins of salmon.
No biscuits. No eggs.
We have plenty of potatoes.

Either as a result of the bombing of shops and food warehouses in Plymouth, or heavy shipping losses that spring, sudden food shortages could occur without warning. This was particularly hard on people like us with nothing in reserve.

One day Gan told us she hadn't been able to get even our basic rations. "We'll just have to make do," she said firmly. "And I don't want to hear any grumbles."

Diane and I looked at one another, askance. Since we never grumbled whatever she put before us, she was obviously preparing us for the worst.

She brought a pie dish from the oven and set it on the bread-board in the middle of the table. It actually looked quite appetising, with only a few burnt bits on its fork-crinkled potato crust. But the look she cast at us was decidedly belligerent. Even Diane knew better than to ask what it was.

Surprisingly, this time she volunteered the information. "It's Toad in the Hole," she announced. "Get it down you." She gave us a large portion each then poured Oxo over it.

Under the top layer of crisp, well-browned potato was another layer mashed, and scattered in this were some Brussels sprouts. "They're meant to be the toads," Gan told us. "It's an old country recipe." We were intrigued and ate it with such relish that she gave it us again, many times. It was years later before I found out that real Toad in the Hole was sausages in batter.

Of course there were many other dishes in which the cook had to forego what might have been considered one of the main ingredients. We had tripe and onions without the onions, which were often in short supply. Gan put in bits of cabbage instead, or carrots, anything she had. Our egg custard tarts never had eggs in them, until the arrival of dried egg from America. They were simply ordinary custard thickened with an extra spoonful of custard powder. And our bread-and-butter pudding was that and nothing more. It never had dried fruit or sugar in it, just a dollop of Gan's blackberry jam on top after it was cooked. These were adaptations every housewife had to make in 1941. But the pseudo Toad in the Hole was one of Gan's more personal and long-lasting culinary deceits.

As spring gave way to summer, a spate of tragedies, national and parochial, hit the village.

The first was the news of the sinking of HMS *Hood*. She had once been based at Devonport Dockyard, manned mainly by Devon and Cornish men. Although she was later transferred to Portsmouth, where docking facilities were more suitable for a ship of her great size, there remained a great deal of feeling for her in the West Country. People wept in the streets when they heard of her loss. All but three of her fourteen hundred men went down with her and Billy Finchcombe was one of them.

Then two village men committed suicide. We didn't know either of them personally, but the daughter of one of them was in my class. When poor Esther came back to school, silent and aloof, we stared at her covertly, as though in some strange way her father's act of despair had branded her.

The most poignant tragedy involved a little boy we knew well. Johnny Penhallow ran fast down Blindwell Hill, eager to get home from school. He couldn't stop at the bottom, and ran straight under a passing lorry. By the time Diane and I, amidst the children thronging down the hill, reached the scene, the vicar was there, called from his church just up the road, and he had covered Johnny's body with his coat. Another adult directed us past in single file, keeping us away from the pathetic little heap in the road. Everyone was shocked and upset by Johnny's death. So many times we had all been told not to run down the one-in-three hill, and he had not been the only child to ignore our teachers' warning.

Sorrow for her neighbour's distress seemed to mellow Gan for a while. She felt a surge of sympathy for Mrs Timble, whose husband was also on a ship, somewhere in the Atlantic, and when they met in a bacon queue in the village, Gan invited her and the children round for a meal, despite us having very little food other than potatoes.

Gan fed us children first, she and Mrs Timble waiting for their meal until Mum came home from the dockyard. It was a meal to remember. For the first time we had bacon, lying on a bed of fried potato, with a circle of mashed carrot around it. And Diane and I were allowed to stay up later to play in the garden with Eva and Garry, while the adults ate.

But the renewal of Gan's 'buddyness' with Mrs Timble did not last. As the year drew nearer to its end and Christmas approached again, Gan suddenly got fed up with inviting the Timbles round.

She said to Mum, in a resentful tone, "Have you noticed how we never get invited round her house?"

We all knew who she meant. Mum tried to head off what she knew was coming. "Well, there are five of us, Mum. There's only three of them."

"What's that got to do with it?" We were ready to go wood-gathering, thickly layered with skirts and jumpers, beneath coats inadequate against the exceptionally cold weather. Gan irritably pushed Diane and me out of the door. "Get a move on, you two. We'll never get out at this rate. As I was saying . . ." She scowled at Mum. "What difference does it make how many are sitting round a fire? It still has to be lit. It still eats wood, and coal when we can get it. *Our* coal, never hers."

Mum sighed. "Stop inviting her then. It's up to you."

Mum's temper was not always as equable as it had been. Tired from the long hours she worked, in a physically exhausting job, she didn't take all Gan's complaints as meekly as she once had.

And Gan, probably just as worn out, flared up at all of us more frequently.

This time she reacted in a way we had not seen before. She retreated into stony silence, ignoring us with such iciness, creating such a repressed atmosphere, we didn't even dare speak to one another, let alone her.

On this occasion, as we reached the police station we saw PC Polworthy.

"Hello, foraging again?" he called cheerfully, eyeing our bags.

Gan couldn't bring herself to answer him. She marched on up the hill, a firm hand dragging Diane with her. I stayed with my hand on the push-chair, ready to help Mum push it.

The policeman gave Mum a knowing look. "Bit testy today, m'dear, is she?"

Mum cast a hasty glance at Gan's rigid back, and Diane's apprehensive face staring back at us over her shoulder. "A bit," she admitted. "I think we're all over-tired."

"Well, you can tell her one bit of news that'll interest her. She was asking last week if I'd heard any more about women police being recruited. Well, it's all off. The decision to take on three of 'em was rescinded at the last hearing. Mind you, it's taken them long enough, best part of a year. But that's one sign things are getting back to normal, tell her."

Mum did not, though. We walked all the way up Donkey Lane, filling our bags to the brim, then made our slow and silent way home without anyone speaking a word. That row seemed to last for ever, certainly well into the next week, because after Mum had gone back to work, Diane and I continued to creep miserably round the house when we came home from school, afraid of saying a word in Gan's hearing.

It proved to be the first of many non-speaking sessions she inflicted on us, and the effect was as devastating as her violent outbursts of temper had been. But at least Diane and I had other children to talk to at school, and each other to whisper to beneath the bedclothes. Poor Jill, often ignored for hours on end when Gan was in one of her moods, grew into a silent little girl, her natural ability to express herself stifled just when it should have been encouraged.

Thankfully, everything seemed to cheer up as preparations for Christmas began. We were better off financially than we had been the previous year. The puddings were hanging in the wash-house, the appetising smell of pudding-cum-mincemeat pies filled the house, and Gan's elderberry wine was ready for drinking.

Tilda came round to confirm the promise of a rabbit on Christmas Eve. She stayed to drink a glass of Gan's wine and it seemed to make her maudlin.

"I had a letter from Greg," she said, her lovely blue eyes blinking back the tears. "He says he thinks of me every night, Mrs Cooper. But he's heard about the bad raids in the South-West and is worrying about Andy and me being on our own. I thought about writing back and telling him his best friend is keeping an eye on us when there's a night raid, to stop him worrying." She hesitated. "But then I thought, perhaps . . . he might . . ."

Gan said grimly, "Yes, he might. So don't!"

"Oh! Well." A note of defiance had crept into Tilda's voice. "He'd be wrong if he did. Because I haven't. Not *really*!"

"Not really?" Gan protested. "And what exactly does that mean, Tilda?"

"What I say! Not really!" Tilda gulped down the rest of her glass of wine and Gan refilled it. "As if I would!"

"Then why give people the chance to *think* you would?"

"I don't! It's not my fault if people think such things. *My* conscience is clear." Two large tears brimmed out of her eyes and rolled down her cheeks.

Gan said hastily, "Get that wine down you and have another."

"I'd better not." Tilda gave a shaky laugh. "That's all I want, for people to say I get tiddly as well." She stood up. "I'll see you tomorrow, with the rabbit, Mrs Cooper. Thanks for the wine, it was lovely."

"Come and have Christmas dinner with us, Tilda," Gan urged. "You'd be very welcome."

"It's kind of you, but the Deweys have already invited us. Don't get up. I'll see myself out."

I had put down my book, where I had been sitting at the corner of the table, reading, to stare in fascination at Tilda's sweetly tragic face.

When she had gone Gan shot me a keen glance and I tensed. But either the spirit of Christmas or her own good wine must have made her genial because her tone wasn't as censorious as I had expected. "Talk about little pitchers having big ears," was all she commented. "You shouldn't have been listening."

She need not have worried. The conversation between her and Tilda had been no more comprehensible to me than if she had invented another secret code.

CHAPTER
NINETEEN

'That old vest . . . use it to a rag then pop it in the bag.'
*(An appeal by the Government for all rags,
even grimy ones, to be handed in to
the Rag and Bone man.)*

As the weather got colder, fuel became more scarce. Worried at the prospect of Christmas without enough to keep our kitchen range going, Mum and Gan had us out collecting wood at every opportunity. Those weekends all through December, we were often out several times a day, to stagger home with loaded bags.

Even Jill did her bit, as she sat uncomplaining in her push-chair, wrapped in her green cape and scarf, to peer from beneath her layer of branches and sticks like some pint-size soldier in camouflage.

Air-raids had eased off and those which occurred were nothing compared to those of the spring blitz. Diane and I, over-excited, finally fell asleep on a quiet Christmas Eve and woke at the crack of dawn, just as children always have on Christmas morning.

We didn't dare get up without Gan's permission, but we crept silently to the end of the bed, where two stockings hung from the bedposts. It was enough simply to explore with inquisitive fingers all the fascinating bumps and crevices in those dark, bulging shapes, before snuggling back under the rag-rug until we were called.

It seemed at first as though it would be the best Christmas ever. With more money we had more presents and Mum's and Gan's cheerfulness set the seal on the happy atmosphere.

Diane, Jill and I all had a new coat each, the first I remember. They were all much too big for us because Gan said we had to have room to grow. But Mum quickly soothed our consternation at sleeves hanging well over our hands and hems down to our ankles.

"I'll turn them up for you before you go back to school," she promised.

Our stockings were filled with presents, *real* presents to us because they were non-essentials. In the toe were an orange and apple. Diane and I then each drew out a skipping-rope, with bells on, a John Bull printing set, a bag of marbles . . . we called them alleys . . . a box of liquorice allsorts and a pack of miniature playing cards. Of all those delights I remember the playing cards giving us the most pleasure, as Mum and Gan taught us to play Patience and Sevens, Snap, Rummy and Strip-Jack-Naked.

Halfway through the morning, when the fire was glowing bright and the wonderful smell of roast rabbit seeped from the oven, we all had a glass of elderberry wine, Diane's and mine watered, Jill's milked. Then Mum started preparing the vegetables and Gan bustled over the range, filling pans with water.

They had just settled at the table again, with another glass of wine, when there came a knock on the door.

There was the usual exchange of dismayed glances between Mum and Gan, the inevitable groan of, "Oh for heaven's sake, who's *that*!" from Gan. This time, her groan contained a hint of hysteria. She looked very uneasy.

"Sssshhhh," she cautioned us. "Keep down." Silently, she crept to the window and peered past the curtain.

She was back in a flash, skidding across the room in one, panic-stricken movement. "Get *down*," she breathed. "It's the Timbles."

For the next five minutes, which seemed more like fifty, she kept us all in varying attitudes of frozen silence, none of us daring to move a finger. Mum had instantly sunk to the floor behind the table, at Gan's urgent gesture, while Diane and I were hustled underneath it. Gan snatched up an open-mouthed Jill, flattened them both against the far wall and fixed Jill's alarmed eyes with her own from an intimidating distance of inches.

"Ssssshhh, Jill," she whispered. "Not a sound," and I don't suppose poor Jill could have uttered one if she had tried.

The Timbles banged on the door several times more, each bang sounding more urgent. I caught a glimpse of Eva peering through the window, before they finally gave up and went away.

We sat another minute or so before Gan ordered, "Upstairs, quick." She made a dash with Jill and we all followed, like shell-shocked sheep.

Upstairs in the back bedroom which Diane and I shared, Gan dumped Jill on the bed and faced a still speechless Mum. "Well, who'd have thought *she* would have the nerve to turn up," she fumed.

Mum stammered, "What . . . ? Why did she . . . ?" then ran out of words.

"You may well ask why," Gan answered grimly. "Because that woman's got the nerve of Old Nick, that's why!"

"But . . . Do you think they had come for Christmas dinner?"

"I'm damn well sure they had. I can't get over *anyone* being so hard-faced!"

"But . . ." Mum seemed as confused as ever. "Why ever should Mrs Timble think they were invited?"

"Because they were. We invited them weeks ago, didn't we? Only I never thought they'd have the neck to turn up, after the way she's treated us."

Mum said slowly, "Mum, are you saying you didn't tell her the invitation was off?"

"No, I did not," Gan exploded. "I gave her credit for enough gumption to *know* it was off. Good Lord, surely she didn't expect us to feed them all, when she can't even invite us round for a cup of tea!"

"Well, it seems she did." It was Mum's turn to be scathing. "So what do we do if they come back?"

Without any hesitation, Gan said, "It won't matter if they do, because we're having our dinner up here."

And that's what we did. While Diane and I sprawled on the bed with Jill and taught her to play Snap, Mum and Gan crept downstairs to serve up our Christmas dinner. They came back up carrying plates full of rabbit and roast potatoes, carrots and peas, all swimming in a wonderful, unusually thick, gravy.

There were no chairs in the bedroom. Mum brought Jill's high-chair upstairs, though she was really getting too big for it, and squeezed her into it. Then she and Gan perched on the edge of the bed with their meals, while Diane and I sat cross-legged on the floor, on the rag-rug, our plates precariously balanced on our legs.

To us children it was all rather exciting to be eating our dinner on the floor. But Mum and Gan didn't seem so thrilled and their subdued spirits hung like a wet blanket over the previously happy atmosphere. It only needed Diane to drop her Christmas pudding and its boiling hot custard onto her bare leg and for Jill to add her howls of sympathy to Diane's yells of pain, for us all to realise that the season of goodwill was over.

That was the end of Christmas 1941. It was the end of our friendship with the Timbles too, for not only did Mrs Timble and Gan never speak to one another again, but Diane and I and Eva felt impelled to ape our elders, and loftily ignored one another for the rest of the time we were to spend in the same school.

Mum's Christmas break was very short and she didn't want it to end, when she would have to go back to work.

Gan, on the other hand, could hardly wait to see the back of Diane and me. She never liked holidays, when we were all under her feet and that Christmas, with bitterly cold weather, and scarcely enough fuel to keep warm, was particularly hard. The tiny cottage must

177

have seemed claustrophobic to her when we were home for days on end, instead of just herself and docile little Jill. We were sent out in the backyard so often, with a no-nonsense order to enjoy ourselves with our new skipping ropes, we were sick of them by the time we went back to school.

Among the highlights in my life were the regular knitting and sewing sessions at Miss Croft's house. She was so kind to me, at a time when I felt unloved at home, I did everything I could to please her. I worked hard enough to become top of her class, every spare moment I had at home I knitted squares for her refugee blankets, from old jumpers she gave me to unravel, and I stopped telling lies.

She talked to me of becoming a teacher one day, like her, and filled me with enthusiasm. It was dented a little when I mentioned my ambition at home. "You don't want to be a teacher," Gan scornfully told me. "They're all old maids." But I secretly kept my dream.

One day, when she had dismissed us at the end of afternoon school, Miss Croft called me back.

"Can you ask your mother if I can come to see her one evening, Betty?" she said, then added quickly, to allay the apprehension I must have betrayed, "It's nothing for you to worry about."

She came one evening, after Diane and I were in bed. Mum and Gan were as mystified as I was about her visit and Mum must have realised I was also in some suspense. She came up to our bedroom after Miss Croft had gone.

178

"It's nothing wrong, Betty," she whispered. "But I can't tell you what it's about because Miss Croft has asked us not to, so there's no chance of you being disappointed. It's something we have to think about. Now, off to sleep like a good girl."

So I was none the wiser, until a change in our circumstances a month or two later made Mum and Gan feel they were released from their promise not to tell.

Not content with falling out with Mrs Timble, Gan had a row in the street with Mrs Dobson, which made Diane and me, on our way home from school, squirm with embarrassment.

We missed the beginning of it. As we came up West Street we could see Mrs Dobson standing facing our house, arms akimbo, and as we got nearer, an angry, red-faced Gan standing on our doorstep. The furious words they were exchanging made our steps falter.

Mrs Dobson's rag-and-bone handcart was parked behind her. A strong, hefty woman, she had always taken her turn collecting scrap, though leaving heavier loads like house removals to her husband.

She was loudly berating Gan. "And you think yourself a respectable woman, trying to cause trouble between a man and his wife? You ought to be ashamed of yourself."

Gan's response was equally heated. "You're potty, woman! I never said a word against your husband. It was *you* who called him a miserable old sod, not me!"

"And what if I did? A wife can say things about her old man and not be out of turn. But nobody else can!"

"I did not say a word against your old man. All I did was agree with you."

"Well, you shouldn't have. It's not your place to agree with something you know nothing about. You should mind your own business, Mrs Cooper."

"Oh, for heaven's sake!" At this point, Gan turned her head and caught sight of us skulking at the corner of Mrs Finchcombe's house. "Come here and get inside," she snapped before her glare slid from us to the house opposite. As she gave us an ungentle shove through the door I caught a glimpse of a face at Mrs Brown's twitching curtains.

As Gan prepared to follow us, Mrs Dobson got in the last word.

"And you can keep your old rags. If they're so mucky you can't even hand them over for the war effort, then heaven help you!"

Gan slammed the door behind us. "All that, just because I didn't want to give her rags I'd used to black-lead the range," she exploded. "Well, that's it. I've had enough."

There was an ominously familiar ring to her words. As though we'd heard them before.

CHAPTER
TWENTY

'On the other side of the Big Black Cloud,
Is the Land where your Dreams come True.'
(*First World War song*)

One weekend, a few weeks after Christmas, Gan told us we were leaving Millbrook. Diane and I stared at her, surprise at first robbing us of the ability to think, let alone say anything.

Mum had taken Jill down to the shops in the village. Gan went on briskly, "Your Mum has been to see a flat in Torpoint and we're moving there next week."

I found my voice first. "But . . . but what about school? Will we still be able to . . . ?"

She firmly interrupted me. "No, of course you won't be able to stay at this school. You'll be going to one in Torpoint. I'll give you a letter to take on Monday, to let your teachers know."

I felt a cold little chill in my stomach. While I stood frozen, trying to take in Gan's words, Diane recovered enough to ask anxiously, "But what about the pencil monitor? Miss Vickerstaff says I can be the next one."

"I'm sorry, Diane, but you can't." Gan still sounded fairly kind, if firm. "I'm sure they'll want pencil monitors in Torpoint School."

My long-gone stammer returned to demoralise me. "B . . . but . . . but . . . I was going to . . . Miss Croft . . . s . . . said . . ."

Whether it was due to the offending stammer, which had always irritated Gan, or the mention of my teacher, whom she had seemed to turn against since Miss Croft's mysterious visit to the house, I drew a sharp rebuke down upon our heads.

She snapped, "Never mind what Miss Croft says. It's what your mother says! She's struggled to the Dockyard and back, week after week, month after month, no matter what the weather's like, or how tired she's been after being up most of the night. She needs to be nearer work. *That's* why we're going to Torpoint. Now don't let me hear any more of your selfish grumbling. Think of your mother for a change."

Neither of us said another word. I could see tears beginning to well in Diane's eyes but she blinked fast and they didn't fall. I withdrew into my own increasingly introverted mind, and kept my dejection inside me.

When I gave Miss Croft my note on Monday morning, I couldn't utter a word of what I felt. I didn't even look at her as she opened it, but slunk to my desk and sat staring at a spill of blotting paper someone had stuck in the ink-well.

I can't remember many details of that last week at Millbrook School, only Miss Croft's unusual reticence towards me. I was too young, and knew too little then, for it to occur to me as it has since that she was probably as upset as I was. And she wasn't a demonstrative woman. Her hurt would have been kept to herself just as mine was. So we never really said goodbye to each other, just a formal little hope from her that I would be happy in my new school, and an equally polite response from me.

I found out, after we *had* left the village, why she had come to see Mum, that evening after school. Mum told me, after I had made some thoughtless remark about Miss Croft falling out with me when she knew I was leaving.

"Don't be unkind about Miss Croft," Mum quietly told me. "She thought a lot of you."

Then she told me of my teacher's offer to be responsible for my education, to pay the fees to send me to a well-known girls' grammar school in Plymouth.

"She said she would also buy your books, if we could just manage your uniform. But we had to tell her we couldn't."

I must have looked stricken. She said gently, "It wouldn't have been fair to Diane and Jill, to give you chances they couldn't have."

Gan wasn't so gentle. "And it wasn't only that, Betty. Your mother and I felt she was getting too big a hold over you. She'd have made you too religious. We don't want any religious maniacs in our family."

When I think about the strange manias Gan had, far more bizarre than the simple belief in prayer which Miss Croft engendered in me, the irony of her words never fails to strike me.

I took the last week's rent to the woman owning our cottage, who lived in a large house near the lake.

"Well, tell your Mum I'm sorry you're leaving, Betty," Mrs Duncan smiled. "I hope my next tenants are as good."

I thought of all the times I had brought the six shillings rent, and how Mrs Duncan had usually given me threepence. Gan had always taken it off me, and had been very put out when occasionally I had been given sweets instead of money.

We *had* been good tenants. Money with which to pay the rent had always been at the top of our list of priorities, with food, fuel and clothes only being bought as we could afford them.

Mrs Duncan was especially generous this time and gave me sixpence. "Goodbye, good luck," she called as she watched me make my way through the white wooden garden gate for the last time.

Gan couldn't have had many goodbyes to make, since she had fallen out with most of her neighbours. She went to see Mrs Finchcombe, still grieving too much over her lost son to care about falling out with anyone. And Mrs Brown, opposite, never having been the type of neighbour to encourage social contact, slowly and silently only left her house when she needed provisions. They were the only two women Gan hadn't had words with.

Mrs Timble had never again darkened our door since Christmas Day, when she and her family had gone home dinnerless. Mrs Dobson, the rag-and-bone lady, haughtily tossed her head every time she met Gan in the village, and Gan did the same to her. And relations with Tilda, which had warmed after she came round about the Christmas rabbit, took a turn for the worse when, during a long-drawn-out manoeuvre with a huge army vehicle outside our two front doors, Tilda got the three soldiers in for a cup of tea before Gan could.

Mr Brown, the air-raid warden, came round to say goodbye. We were all there. Diane and I had been allowed to stay up later every night in that last week, perhaps as a kind of consolation for being uprooted with less than a week in which to come to terms with it. Gan offered him a cup of tea but he hadn't time to stop.

"I'm sorry to hear you're leaving, Mrs Cooper," the kindly old man told her before looking at Mum and lowering his voice a tone.

"I hope you're not taking your little family into the lion's den, m'dear," he said soberly. "The raids do seem to have eased off but that's not to say we won't get any more. Torpoint is too near the Dockyard for my liking."

Before Mum could answer Gan cut in. "But that's just why we're going there, so Ida won't have so far to travel."

Mr Brown was looking at Mum, very concerned. "Them Nazis only have to miss Devonport you know, and Torpoint gets it. Whereabouts are you going to live?"

Mum told him, "Clarence Road. There's been no bombing near there, and it's walking distance from the ferry," and at the same time Gan said:

"And Mrs Finchcombe was telling me they always go for the Naval Camp, and that's nowhere near Clarence Road."

"Well, at least you're not near the navy camp, that's one blessing. But you know, the ferry's had a number of near misses." Mr Brown shook his head. "But you can always come back to Millbrook, m'dear, if Torpoint gets too hot for you."

"Oh no we won't." But Gan's exasperated denial was firmly blocked out by Mum's hearty reply.

"Of course we could, Mr Brown," she smiled. "But I'm sure we're going to be very happy in our new flat."

On the way out, Mr Brown gave Gan's hand a goodbye pat. He did as he always did when speaking to her. Inexplicably, he raised his voice and slowed his words.

"It's been a pleasure, Mrs Cooper," he boomed. "I'm sorry you're going. I shall miss our little chats."

Unlike her usual exchanges with Mr Brown, Gan made herself both seen and heard.

She made a gracious little farewell speech.

"Thank you for all your help, Mr Brown. If ever you and your wife are in the Torpoint area, do call in for a cup of tea. It's the bottom flat, thirty-five, Clarence Road . . . thirty-five . . . thirty-five Clarence Road. Did you get that?"

Mr Brown seemed surprised. His voice took on a gentle, humouring tone. "Now anybody would think you're suggesting I'm getting a bit hard of hearing, Mrs Cooper." He wagged a finger at her.

Gan's good humour was less gentle than determined.

"It's surprising how some people always get the wrong end of the stick, isn't it," she said, quite affably. "And I'm neither deaf nor daft, no matter what some folk seem to think."

The unwavering smile on her lips, yet with no warmth at all in the glassy-eyed stare she fixed on the poor man, put Mr Brown completely off balance. He didn't know how to take her and turned a rather helpless glance on Mum.

She didn't fail him.

"I think we're all getting a bit the worse for wear these days, Mr Brown," she soothed. "Even the kids are showing signs." She had walked him to the door before needing to elaborate.

Standing by the window, I heard what passed between Mum and the warden as she saw him out.

"She's a bit . . . you know?" she whispered and he whispered back:

"I thought that was it, m'dear. Never you fret. I understand."

Which was more than I did. But one thing was for sure. Gan couldn't have caught what had been said, or Mum wouldn't have got away with it.

On the evening before we left, Gan could hardly wait for Mum coming home, before pouring out a bitter grievance which had been rankling inside her all afternoon.

"You'll never credit this," she started before Mum had got her coat off. "I met Mrs Pendennis in the village and do you know what that woman has had the nerve to say about us?"

"Who, Mrs Pendennis?" Mum wearily shrugged off her coat and flopped onto a chair at the table.

"No, of course not," Gan said irritably. "Though I'm surprised she had the face to repeat such a scandalous tale, and I told her what I thought of her for it. I mean Madam Timble."

She paused to draw an indignant breath. Mum asked, resignedly, "All right, what *has* she accused us of?"

"She's accused us of being lice-ridden, that's what she's accused us of." Gan need not have doubted the effect of her words. Mum was horrified.

"Lice-ridden?" she repeated in disbelief.

Gan's voice throbbed with indignation. "She told Mrs Pendennis that the reason she had fallen out with us . . . *she* had fallen out, if you please . . . was because they had picked up a bug when they slept at our house during the bad raids. When I think of all we did for that

188

woman and her snotty-nosed kids! Well, I'm going to have it out with her before we go."

"Oh Mum, don't! It's not worth it." Even Gan in her righteous anger must have heard the weariness in Mum's voice, seen it in her face. "What does it matter? We're leaving, going to make a fresh start. Let's just forget about the Timbles and the Dobsons, Tilda Hawkins and Mrs Pendennis." She was so tired, her voice quivered over their names, but she managed a smile. "How about a cup of tea, Mum? I'm parched."

For once, Gan knew when to stop. "Yes, let's have a cup of tea," she agreed. "You're right, Ida. I've never met such a quarrelsome set of women, always ready to take offence no matter how much I've tried to be pleasant, all of 'em full of old buck. I'll be glad to get out."

And that was the aura our impending move to Torpoint seemed to take on. It had an element of escape, a feeling of getting out of town. A fresh start. A whole new lot of people for Gan to fall out with. We caught some of her sense of relief, were lifted to optimism by her determined good humour.

Now, she forgot about the tea and brought out a bottle of her latest damson wine, watering Diane's and mine, milking Jill's and pouring out a large glassful each for herself and Mum.

"There, get that down you," she told us all. She held up her glass of rich red wine.

"Well, here's to Torpoint, Ida," she toasted. "May it be the best move we've ever made," and she drank it to the dregs.

ISIS publish a wide range of books in large print, from fiction to biography. Any suggestions for books you would like to see in large print or audio are always welcome. Please send to the Editorial department at:

ISIS Publishing Ltd.
7 Centremead
Osney Mead
Oxford OX2 0ES
(01865) 250 333

A full list of titles is available free of charge from:
Ulverscroft large print books

(UK)
The Green
Bradgate Road, Anstey
Leicester LE7 7FU
Tel: (0116) 236 4325

(Australia)
P.O Box 953
Crows Nest
NSW 1585
Tel: (02) 9436 2622

(USA)
1881 Ridge Road
P.O Box 1230, West Seneca,
N.Y. 14224-1230
Tel: (716) 674 4270

(Canada)
P.O Box 80038
Burlington
Ontario L7L 6B1
Tel: (905) 637 8734

(New Zealand)
P.O Box 456
Feilding
Tel: (06) 323 6828

Details of **ISIS** complete and unabridged audio books are also available from these offices. Alternatively, contact your local library for details of their collection of **ISIS** large print and unabridged audio books.